Advance Praise for
Angels and Entrepreneurs

"My wife and I have been dear friends with Bob and Myrna Schlegel for more than twenty-five years, dating back to my days filming the *Walker, Texas Ranger* television series in Dallas. In fact, our twins were ring bearers at his oldest daughter's wedding. Although Bob has yet to master my signature roundhouse kick, he has many other talents. I've watched him grow his very successful companies over the years and he is truly a natural born entrepreneur. And so, this book is a great resource for others nourishing an entrepreneurial spirit as well as a philanthropic heart and the desire to use their God-given talents to serve others. *Angels and Entrepreneurs* will inspire you and light the way for you!"

—Chuck Norris

"I know talent when I see it. Talent is great. But what really separates talent from success is perseverance, determination, and hard work. Bob is the perfect example of that. He took his God-given strengths and worked hard, never giving up when things were challenging. In this book, Bob coaches you through some tough plays and shares what he has learned through his wins and losses. He is a man of great character, strength, and generosity as evidenced in the stories throughout this book. This book is a WIN!"

—Jerry Jones, Owner, President and General Manager of the Dallas Cowboys

"*Angels and Entrepreneurs* is an inspiring book sharing the lessons learned and ups and downs all entrepreneurs will inevitably face while navigating business, relationships, and life. A must-read, not only to learn how to make money and be successful in business, but also how to build a life filled with gratitude and healthy relationships."

—Jim Treliving, member of *Dragons' Den* and owner
of Boston Pizza North American Franchisor

"A must-read inspirational journey on the road of life. A story of love, passion, and perseverance...and the American Dream!"

—Jeffrey A. Rich, former CEO of Affiliated
Computer Systems (ACS)

"My friend Bob Schlegel tells it like it is. If you've ever thought of becoming an entrepreneur or if you are just curious about what makes entrepreneurs do what they do, this is a must-read. If you are already an entrepreneur, you can take Bob's hard-earned lessons to the bank."

—Craig Hall, Real Estate and Wine Entrepreneur
and *New York Times* bestselling author

"I may be biased because I count Bob and Myrna among my closest friends, but Bob's life story of drive, tenacity, and self-reliance is a wonderful story. Entrepreneurs are a fascinating breed, and I never tire of hearing their inspiring examples of hard work and determination. It is incumbent upon all of us to cultivate and nurture the entrepreneurial drive in others, for they are our future."

—Trisha Wilson, Founder and retired CEO of Wilson Associates
Hospitality Design Firm, and the Wilson Foundation

"*Angels and Entrepreneurs* is the perfect title for a Bob Schlegel book...because he is both! The consummate angel and entrepreneur, Bob has never known a stranger or a failure. Every stranger is turned into a friend, and every failure into a learning experience.

Bob has served as an inspiration to me and will be a guiding light, both personally and professionally, for all who read the book."

—Jim Keyes, Jim Keyes, Retired CEO 7-Eleven Corporation
and founder, Education is Freedom Foundation

"For more than two decades, I have watched Bob successfully balance the integrated aspects of faith, family, and business. This book is inspiring in that it captures the essence of the building blocks of his success including his roots, his perseverance, and his indomitable spirit."

—Brian Derksen, CPA Retired Deputy CEO, Deloitte

"Growing hugely successful companies while always putting his family first, Bob Schlegel's entrepreneurial journey and well-rounded lifestyle has long been an inspiration to me. Bob has given me valuable advice in business, relationships, family, and more. This book filled with his and Myrna's stories and lessons will help readers pave the path of successful and meaningful entrepreneurship."

—Jeff Sinelli, Founder and Chief Vibe Officer,
Which Wich Superior Sandwiches

ANGELS
AND
ENTREPRENEURS

A LIFESTYLE FORMULA
for STARTING YOUR OWN BUSINESS
and RIDING the ROLLERCOASTER
of ENTREPRENEURSHIP

BOB SCHLEGEL

SAVIO
REPVBLIC

A SAVIO REPUBLIC BOOK
An Imprint of Post Hill Press
ISBN: 978-1-63758-151-3
ISBN (eBook): 978-1-63758-152-0

Angels and Entrepreneurs:
A Lifestyle Formula for Starting Your Own Business and Riding the
Rollercoaster of Entrepreneurship
© 2022 by Bob Schlegel
All Rights Reserved

posthillpress.com
New York • Nashville
Published in the United States of America

2 3 4 5 6 7 8 9 10

This book is dedicated to my father, a natural born entrepreneur even if he never used the term, and to my mother who pushed me to go beyond my dream of being a gas station pump jockey, and complete high school and college instead. And finally, also to my wife/business partner and our entrepreneurial children. Without their inspiration and encouragement this book would not exist.

Table of Contents

Chapter One

ANGELS AND ENTREPRENEURS

After more than thirty years building two industry-leading businesses from the ground up, my wife Myrna and I found all that we'd worked so hard to accomplish threatened by our bankers and their lawyers in 2009.

Two factors beyond our control had brought the wolves to our door. A surprise government ruling halted our plan to sell our most successful start-up, the landscape materials manufacturer Pavestone Company, for $540 million. Then, the Great Recession hit, dramatically driving down the value of that company.

I had borrowed more than $200 million in loans that were partially guaranteed by me personally. I used that money to finance the growth of Pavestone, which included the construction of sixteen concrete plants across the country. When the federal government stopped the sale and then the global economy plunged, the banks began demanding their money and threatening to seize everything we owned. It was a perfect storm!

We were blindsided and sent reeling by this one-two punch. Myrna and I will always remember this as the most challenging period of our lives.

I refused to declare bankruptcy out of a sense of obligation and honor. We had to sell off other businesses that we'd built with our children to help them in their own entrepreneurial careers. We also cut back on our philanthropy.

We fought through it, rose above it, and got over it. Thanks to the angels in our lives.

I will write in much greater depth about that epic struggle and ultimate victory in our family's entrepreneurial career later in this book. I shared a bit of that story here because I want you to understand that my goal is to provide you with a full understanding of both the ups and downs of creating, building, and owning your own businesses.

My family and I have had a blast, and we are still deeply involved in entrepreneurial endeavors that, most recently, have been challenged by the global pandemic, as well as all of the economic upheaval that has accompanied it in the dawn of a new decade.

We are still in the game because even as immigrants from Canada, we believe in the American dream. We have seen that its capitalistic system offers the world's greatest opportunities for self-betterment and fulfillment. Yet, the accumulation of wealth and material things is not what drives us—and my hope is that it will not be what drives you in your endeavors, either.

Our purpose in building every business is to develop a strong foundation for our family, create jobs and contribute to economic growth in our communities and our countries, and to provide products and services that fill societal needs to elevate the lives of all.

Most of all, my message to all entrepreneurs and aspiring entrepreneurs is that you should always build your businesses for your family, with your family, and around your family. The greatest reward, at the end of each day and at the end of your career, is having someone to support you in the hard times and share the joy with you in the good times.

Believe me, I have known both, and I never would have survived—or *wanted* to survive—without my family and friends, the angels in my entrepreneurial life.

SHARING THE BLESSINGS

You may have seen the title of this book and wondered, "What do angels and entrepreneurs have in common?"

Maybe you've known entrepreneurs who weren't exactly angels.

Or perhaps you've never thought of angels running a start-up.

The angels referred to in the title and throughout this book are simply the wonderful people and other blessings I've had in my life and my career as an entrepreneur, including those from the spiritual world—the Holy Spirit and my guardian angels, as well as the Lord above.

I am an optimist by nature, and a big believer in the power of positive thinking, which has been identified as a key entrepreneurial trait in many books and studies over the decades.

Lady Luck may also have played a role in our family's success. And I have to say that in some cases, those who appeared to be enemies turned out to actually be blessings in disguise—even though that may not have been their intention. The old saying "What goes around comes around" applies to those situations. Also, sometimes you just need to thank God for unanswered prayers.

My cast of angels watching over and guiding me includes family, friends, and business associates, as well as those heavenly spirits who've guided me and strengthened me in challenging times.

Though I have yet to see one of them, I believe in the heavenly angels because without them, I never could have survived all the near-death experiences and business calamities I've been through. Nor could I have enjoyed such a loving family and blessed life.

I've written this book to share those blessings, and to inspire and encourage you and all dreamers and disrupters to start, grow, and reap the rewards of your own enterprises. In the following pages, I will provide you with the nuts and bolts, the nitty-gritty of cash flow and market share, as well as the hard-earned lessons I've learned over more than fifty years as an entrepreneur in a wide range of fields.

I've made a lot of money with successful businesses. I've also gone through times when it looked like I might lose both my businesses and my wealth. I survived those difficult and scary times because my family and friends rallied around me. My angels.

You, too, will need angels by your side if you are to succeed in business and reap the full financial and personal rewards of your efforts. You will need the love and support of a life partner, family, friends, and other individuals, and also those unseen guardians who will show up in the darkest of times and guide you through.

My advice, then, is to recruit your own angels as avidly as you recruit business partners, great team members and long-term customers and clients. Build trusting and mutually supportive relationships by treating everyone you encounter with humility, respect, honesty, and kindness.

I believe that if you share your gifts unselfishly and focus on serving others as you build your business, you will have no regrets. That doesn't mean you should allow anyone to take advantage of you or steal from you, however. I've been known to play hardball when the situation demands it, but my goal with every deal is to be fair with everyone involved by creating win-win situations.

Do not make the mistake of thinking that the entrepreneurial life is just about building a pile of money, though. That is a recipe for a lonely life, even if you end up with a mountain of cash.

For me and most of my entrepreneurial friends and family members, creating businesses is about using our talents and energy to build something of value that benefits our families and our employees, while also impacting our communities and our world in a positive way.

I've known a few driven entrepreneurs who've attained enormous wealth only to wonder why their palatial homes and expensive collections of cars and wine haven't brought them the joy and peace they felt they deserved. They'd worked hard and succeeded on many levels, except when it came to their relationships—and their souls.

Without the angels in my life, I might have become one of those lonely entrepreneurs. Without my family and friends, their love, trust, and support—and their occasional challenges to my way of thinking—I would never have survived the obstacles that come with starting, growing, and running diverse companies.

USE YOUR GIFTS TO SERVE A HIGHER PURPOSE

Most people will tell you that I'm a numbers guy. My biggest strength as an entrepreneur is a gift for compiling and interpreting financial data. My kids call me "the human calculator."

And they know my weaknesses. In 2005, my daughter convinced me to organize, arrange, and manage the seating plan for her wedding with 1,200 guests by putting it on a spreadsheet. She knew that I love playing with them, and it helped us track the ever-changing list, thanks to guest preferences and schedule shifts.

I got even more experience at handling wedding arrangements for guests at another daughter's wedding. I somehow had to figure out how to strategically seat three guests who were running against each other in a primary for the U.S. Senate! They didn't want to be anywhere near each other, so that was tricky to chart.

Yet I am not just about business transactions. I grew up in a small Canadian Mennonite farming community, surrounded by many uncles, aunts, cousins, and other close-knit families. Our rural outpost was focused on faith, family, and work.

Service to others was central to our beliefs and part of our daily lifestyle. If someone's barn was damaged by a storm or a fire, the neighbors from miles around would come together for a barn raising, using their collective skills and efforts. No one had to ask or beg for help; this was just the way we lived.

We knew that by joining forces and working together we could accomplish more than any one of us could do alone. Our goal was to build enterprises and organizations that would support our families and benefit the community as a whole by providing jobs and elevating lives.

My wife and business partner Myrna (my true angel) and I both grew up with that mindset. Throughout this book, I will encourage you to think of the good you can do and the positive impact you can make, more than the money you can collect or the things you can buy with it.

Don't get me wrong, I'm all for building wealth and providing comforts for your loved ones. But no one makes it on their own. And at the end of your life, you don't want to find yourself alone because you were focused on individual success or financial success rather than building mutually supportive and loving relationships.

A key word to keep in mind as you read this book, and as you go about building your own businesses and entrepreneurial life, is gratitude. If you always carry gratitude in your heart, no problems will seem insurmountable, and even the smallest blessing will lighten your load.

And when you have gratitude in your heart as an entrepreneur, you will be drawn, as I am, to opportunities that serve a greater purpose and benefit the world around you.

Do your best and prepare for the worst

There are risks in any enterprise. You can't escape them. Usually the higher the risks, the greater the rewards—if all goes well. But I can attest that there will be times when you just won't know what hit you.

A change in government regulations. A global recession. Who would have thought a global pandemic could still change the world overnight? A sudden leap in technology that transforms your industry. An overpowering competitor. A sudden threat to your health, or the crippling loss of a loved one.

Forces beyond your control will bring you to your knees. I've made millions of dollars with my businesses. And, as noted earlier, I've also stood teetering on the precipice of financial disaster.

I've watched my wife shed tears as our creditors gathered around a huge conference table trying to scare the bleep out of us. It worked! They had dozens of lawyers present, threatening to seize everything for which we'd worked for over thirty years.

Be warned: You may have similar moments as an entrepreneur. And you will need angels if you are to survive them. So do not neglect your relationships. Fortify yourself with a foundation of faith, family, and community.

There is another key point that I want to make up front in this book. Many entrepreneurs will tell you that it is impossible to find "balance" between your work life and your family life.

I believe that is absolutely true. However, I also believe it's just the wrong approach. Your work life and your family life should not be separate levels of existence. Frankly, I think that's impossible to pull off. I don't feel you have to compartmentalize your life in that manner.

Myrna and I worked side by side for many years. We never tried to separate work from home. Our dinner table conversations with our children always included open and candid discussions of our business matters, both the good and the bad.

If one of us, or both of us, had to miss something in our children's lives, we made sure they understood that it was only because we were working for their long-term benefit, too. As they grew older, our kids accompanied us on business trips, and they even sat in on negotiations from time to time.

Now, as adults, all four of them own and operate their own enterprises with our full support. We didn't push them to do that. We only pushed them to do their best and make the most of their opportunities.

Though we never tried to guide their career choices, our three daughters and our son often credit Myrna and me with inspiring them by example. To my gratitude and delight, they all agree that one of their sources of day-to-day inspiration is a simple phrase that I said to each of them after we said goodbye as I dropped them off at school: "Be good. Work hard. I love you."

My dream for this book is that you and others will read it and be inspired and prepared to build meaningful lives that include financial success.

More importantly, I hope you will attract and appreciate those angels in your life who encourage you to be good, work hard, and know that you are loved.

Many of my entrepreneur friends comment on the unusual bond that Myrna and I have had as both business partners and life partners. My friend, Jim Keyes, former 7-Eleven and Blockbuster CEO, said recently of my relationship with Myrna, "Rarely do you find a life partner, lover, and best friend who is also a trusted business associate. It is a very precious thing to have, and you make a great team.

"It is obvious that you and Myrna place a lot of value on relationships and family," he added. "I think that is because you met very young and became friends, grew up together and became lovers, and then business partners. Yet you've never lost an ounce of the passion that has led to your success on every level, including growing an entire family of entrepreneurs."

ROOTS OF ENTREPRENEURSHIP

If you picked up this book because you need more income or want more independence and control over your destiny, then you've come to the right place. Most of the entrepreneurs I've known are bootstrappers who started out with very little but built businesses and wonderful lives thanks to their own hard work, determination, and optimistic attitudes—and the occasional intervention of an angel or two.

The same holds true for me, though, as you will discover, I may have been rescued by angels more times than most. I was born into a humble, working-class family on a 160-acre farm about sixty miles west of Toronto, Canada, in the middle of the Great Lakes region.

Our bit of land was near my grandfather's original family farm just outside a hamlet with the unique name of Punkeydoodles Corners. That land was granted to our Schlegel ancestors by the British Crown in 1839—twenty-eight years before Canada became independent of Britain. To get the land grant, *all* they had to do was agree to clear the trees and rocks, brush from the land, and grow crops. Oh yeah, *and* dig water wells, *and* build houses and barns— from the trees they had to cut down. It would be another one hundred years before electricity was available in our region. My father "wired" the farm and installed the electricity himself.

Over the years, the original farm was cut up, with sections of it doled out to family heirs and descendants. Many of my cousins still have farms around the old village area, which can be hard to find because strangers with an affinity for funny place names keep stealing the Punkeydoodle signs.

I am grateful to have grown up in the country, but many people have idealized visions of farm life. The work is hard. The hours are long. And farmers are at the mercy of many elements beyond their control.

Yes, farming is the original entrepreneurial job. But if you just coast along, doing the bare minimum, you will fail. No one else will get up and do the farm chores or feed the livestock for you. And if the chickens aren't fed, they tend to peck each other to death. That's not a good thing.

On the other hand, if you work as hard as your farm neighbors, produce more eggs and grain, and stay at least one step ahead of the bankers and the government regulators, you can reap the full rewards of your efforts—minus taxes and chicken feed costs.

Do not be mistaken, however: Owning your own business is fraught with dangers. This is another lesson I learned on the farm. Many city people see the beauty of the countryside and think it's all spacious skies and amber waves of grain.

They forget that farming is often listed as one of the most dangerous occupations. You are working with heavy machinery, chemical fertilizers, and weed killers, along with messy and unpredictable livestock.

I've known farmers who were badly injured or even killed on the job. You learn to trust in the angels because there are so many factors out of your control, including the weather, government regulation, erratic farm animals, and heavy equipment that can be hazardous to operate.

When I was in ninth grade, our live-in farmhand was killed when the tractor he was driving flipped over. I always remember this because he teased me at breakfast just before going out to work. It was the anniversary of D-Day in World War II, and he joked that it was *my* D-Day, too, because that was the day my classmates and I were told which final exams we would be exempt from writing (or, in my case, the exams I would *not* be exempt from writing).

An hour after school started, the vice principal came into my class and asked me to come with him. My mother was in his office. She told me then that Dave had been killed in a tractor accident on the farm. She hadn't wanted me to hear it from anyone else because she knew when I found out about the loss of my dear friend, I would be terribly distraught.

CLOSE CALLS

Growing up on a farm, there were hazards everywhere, and I seemed to find them all. I barely made it out of my childhood alive. I still have several scars on my body from the stitches it took to sew me up many times. I received my first stitches after I rode down our high metal slide in a barrel and cut my head open. Then, when I was five years old, I fell off a piece of farm equipment I'd been playing on and had a much more serious injury.

I landed on my butt and hit hard, but it didn't really hurt at first. Being young and clueless, I didn't tell anyone about the fall until they noticed that I was holding my head in a strange way, several days later.

"Bobby, why are you holding your neck at such an odd angle?" my mom had asked.

I had to confess then that I'd fallen, and the pain seemed to be getting worse in my back and neck.

The next thing I knew, I was in the hospital, hanging from my chin while a team of doctors and nurses wrapped the upper half of my body like a mummy. Only my face and arms were visible!

I started grade one in that body cast, in a one-room schoolhouse. I instantly stood out from the three other kids in my grade, though maybe not for the right reasons. I did get a lot of autographs on the cast, though.

My brother said I looked like a Martian. My doctors said I was lucky to be alive. I'd broken my neck and compressed my spine somehow. I could have been paralyzed for life. I wore the cast for six months and it took another three or four months before I no longer moved like a robot in dire need of a lube job.

Looking back on that incident, I had to think there was an angel watching out for me. For a couple days after the fall, I did my farm chores and pretty much all the normal kid stuff without realizing I had a broken neck. No one could figure out why I wasn't crippled.

Thankfully, my guardian angel stayed on duty, because I had another close call a while later. This time my guardian angels joined forces with my older brother Don.

I was seven years old. Our parents were attending a weekly prayer meeting at our church, about five miles from our farmhouse. It was wintertime and I was home with Don, who was seventeen, and our sister Mary, who was twelve.

As I recall, I saw smoke coming up through a floor vent. I hollered and Don came running. He then ran downstairs to the cellar and saw the fire was down there. He went hunting for the fire extinguisher.

I was too impatient to wait for him, so I filled a bowl with water from the kitchen sink and ran down to the basement to be the hero who saved the family home.

My heroic dreams died when I ran into a wall of flames. I threw my water on it, to no effect, and scrambled back up the stairs. My brother and sister dragged me outside. Only a couple walls and a small section of the second floor survived the fire. The roof was gone.

Several days after the fire died out, I joined my dad and several neighbors and we tried to salvage furniture on the second floor. Our search was interrupted when someone screamed, "Look out! It's falling!"

We were all thrown to the floor as that last remaining section of the house started tilting in slow motion as a support wall collapsed. It was my dad's turn to be my guardian angel. He grabbed me by my shirt collar as we were thrown to the floor and held me tight as we somehow slid safely to the ground level, along with the volunteers helping to salvage what could be saved.

My parents were still rebuilding the farmhouse that summer when I had an even more harrowing experience. We were living in a small apartment created as our temporary quarters above the farm's equipment workshop. It was a beautiful sunny day, and I was playing outside with Don's two Great Danes, Buddy and Olly.

They had always been good dogs. I had played with them often without ever having a problem. On this day, though, something set them off like never before.

I was playfully rolling on the ground with them, as usual, but when I tried to crawl away from them, they both came after me in a frenzy. I'd never heard them bark and growl so aggressively. Then they tore into me, biting me all over my body, tossing me around and dragging me through the dirt.

As this mauling continued, Don drove by on the tractor in a field close by. At first, he thought his dogs had gotten hold of a small animal or a red bag that they were tearing up. Then, in horror, he realized it was his bloodied little brother being attacked.

Then he jumped off the tractor, ran over, and pulled me away from his dogs. I was bleeding from bites and clawings and bruised all over. My mom drove me to the hospital, where they dressed the wounds and stitched me up.

I spent another several days there recovering. I still have scars from that day. The attack of the Great Danes was a very scary experience, but honestly, after I started my own businesses, I suffered much worse mauling by lenders and partners.

Before entering my teen years, I had yet another life-threatening experience—less violent, but still scary. When I was about nine years old, I spent a Sunday playing with a cousin, who was still a baby and just learning to walk.

What made this particular Sunday fun day so frightening and memorable for all of us was what happened over the days that immediately followed. The day after we played together, my cousin wasn't feeling well. He became feverish and nauseous, experiencing muscle weakness and neck pain. Within a week, he could barely control his limbs.

Doctors finally diagnosed him with polio, a highly contagious virus that had been mostly eradicated thanks to a vaccine perfected by Jonas Salk in 1955.

After my cousin was diagnosed, my parents and all the community prayed for my cousin, as well as me and the other children in our rural area who had been around him. It was a time similar to the coronavirus outbreak around the world. Mom and Dad monitored our every move for weeks and months after they realized we had been exposed to the polio virus, but once again, my angels were protecting us.

We don't know how my cousin contracted it, but he never regained the use of his limbs. He lived a good life despite challenges, dying at age sixty-two.

AN ENTREPRENEUR IN THE MAKING

My father, LeRoy, was born in 1914 and was a teenager during the Great Depression. That made him very aware of creating financial security and the dangers of changing financial markets. He was from a multigenerational dairy farm family that had been on the land since 1839.

He was a dairy farmer originally. Later on, he switched from raising dairy cows to raising turkeys, hogs, and chickens. To supplement his farm income, he went to trade school and learned to be an electrician and a plumber.

Electricity was just coming to the farms in our rural area in Southern Canada in those days. I've often had people there tell me that my dad wired their family's farm to provide it with electricity for the first time. Additionally, most of them needed indoor plumbing, including toilets, in their homes, and my dad also provided running water for them for the first time.

My father was a true entrepreneur. I don't know how he found time for all of his jobs. He also started and operated a Massey Ferguson farm equipment dealership and repair garage with an attached gas station. When he hired his first licensed auto mechanic and paid him $100 a week, I thought to myself, *I want that job!*

I saw how hard my father worked, so I wanted to do my share. At the age of thirteen, I started working there as a grease monkey and doing my dream job of pumping gas for several summers. I did that along with my early morning and after-school farm chores. I looked for other ways to earn money, too. I ordered garden and flower seeds from catalogs and sold them. I also became a distributor for a nice brand of jackknives, which were popular with my woodsmen buddies.

My drive to make extra cash grew more ambitious in my teen years. I bought a Pepsi machine from a local distributor under an agreement in which I paid off the loan over three years at twelve dollars a month with the proceeds, and then kept the profits after that. The soda machine was located in my father's implement repair shop and turned out to be a profitable venture where I learned about cash flow and fixed costs (twelve dollars a month), as well as variable marginal income of three cents on a ten-cent Pepsi bottle. I learned early about break-even sales. I needed to sell 400 bottles each month to do that.

I can't say that things worked out so well for another of my businesses, which I started when I was seventeen. I was talking to my dad and a friend of his one day when the friend told me that he'd bought into a multilevel marketing company that sold a hot new product called "Car Bar."

He explained that it was a system you put under the car dashboard with gizmos that had cupholders. It hooked up a manifold to the car's radiator lines so you could make hot water, coffee, and soup in your vehicle. The system also included a big icebox for cold drinks in the car's trunk. There was a control button mounted on the dashboard, and you could put a coffee cup under a spout on your dash, then push the button and make soup and coffee or hot water for whatever you wanted, kind of like a modern-day Keurig under your dash. Excellent for wining and dining my dates!

"You ought to get in on this too, Bobby," my dad's friend said. "All the new cars will soon have them."

I noticed that my father, who was sitting behind his friend, was shaking his head "no" to try and warn me off, but I was already sold. "What could possibly go wrong? I'll take the minimum three to start," I said.

The buy-in was $360, which was all my savings. I pitched the Car Bars to friends, family members, and anyone I could get to listen. "By 1970, every car in America will have one of these!"

I sold one to our neighbor, and another to a milk truck driver. I put the third one in my own car because I couldn't find anyone else who wanted it. The concept seemed promising, but in reality, it was a lot easier to stop at a drive-in, or just to make your coffee and soup in the house, put it in a cooler, and eat it when you were ready.

I thought this great idea would sell millions, but it didn't. I had to chalk it up to a learning experience. I learned to make sure there is a market for your product before going into business. It was a valuable lesson, and at that time, it didn't cost me all that much, but it would pay off handsomely in the years that followed. This was my first lesson in making sure never to invest in any business before I understood its market. Another little obvious tip: Don't take advice from someone trying to sell you something.

SHIFTING ECONOMICS

I learned another important lesson while growing up: Any changes in government regulations or the economy can have a big impact on any business. So, you have to constantly keep an eye out for looming storms while being ready, willing, and able to adjust and adapt to a changing environment. That is why my businesses do SWOT analysis these days—that is, we look for Strengths, Weaknesses, Opportunities, and Threats. Whoever would have thought that a global virus like Covid-19 could affect business in the world as it has? But keep in mind that you also need to be on the corner when the bus stops, by which I mean, prepared for opportunities.

During my childhood there was a big population shift in Canada from rural areas to urban centers. Many struggling small farms were bought up and merged to create much larger and more efficient operations. As this was happening, the costs of feed and fuel soared, as did just about everything else we needed to keep the place going.

Government quotas limited the number of livestock you could have, which made it very difficult to expand a farm. Canada's climate isn't the best for livestock, either, especially poultry in the summer. Our turkeys were allowed to roam the range, and one year we lost half the flock due to intense rains and flooding. These hard times put my family on the edge in my teen years.

I accompanied my father on several trips to ask our local bank for loans to keep the farm operating. It was humbling, but because we lived in a close-knit small town, the bankers were usually sympathetic. They never foreclosed on us, but the threat was always there.

I learned that it pays to stay friendly with bankers, but later, I would discover that was easier to do in a rural community, where everyone knew everyone and most of us belonged to the same churches. Even so, you can't keep a farm operating if all of your profits go to the interest on your loans.

My parents, relatives, and friends were very social people, active in the church and the community. They often helped out elderly people in our town, bringing them groceries, doing repairs to their homes, and caring for them when they were sick. My folks were among many townspeople who sponsored refugees from Europe after WWII. They helped them get job training and places to live so they could start a new life in Southern Ontario.

Everyone looked out for each other, and that philosophy included working together to find ways through difficult financial times. All of my parent's siblings were farmers. One of them also was a minister, and he started a rehabilitation hospital for the elderly as a mission for his church several years earlier. It was in a neighboring town, and I visited there many times as a boy.

Then, in 1967, as part of another community outreach mission, my dad's brother recruited him, another brother, and two friends to invest in a London-area residential center for the elderly. They bought an abandoned Catholic nunnery about an hour from our home, renovated it, and created a licensed nursing facility.

The plan was for the five of them to raise $10,000 each to buy and renovate the vacant property. My dad had to borrow his share from a church friend in the U.S. who was a successful businessman, and who also bought a share.

This was a big deal for everyone in our extended family, so our parents filled us in on every aspect of the deal. You might say it was my first lesson in serious business investment and arranging the capital stack. It also turned out to be a very good lesson on return on investment and leveraging your money. A year or two later, my dad sold their share back to his brothers for a good multiple of their original investment, and then started their own nursing retirement center in a former schoolhouse in Tavistock, which was my father's hometown.

They learned that when operated correctly, businesses could be very successful, thanks to the socialized medicine program in Canada at the time. For people of our faith, it was also a way to do well by doing good and make a positive impact on the lives of others.

Helping others was part of our core belief system, and there were few things as rewarding as developing a facility to care for our residents and seeing how much it benefitted the elderly in our town.

My parents actually moved off our farm and into the nursing facility as live-in managers while I was still a teenager, leaving me to live there on my own for my last years of high school.

I could see that farming was not my destiny, however. The tradition was for the oldest son to take over the farm, and my brother was glad to do that. I decided to follow in the footsteps of someone my father had relied on over the years as he tried to keep the farm going.

Jim Roth would come visiting once a year because he was my dad's tax accountant, a CPA (Certified Public Accountant). My parents were always glad to see him, so he seemed like someone who helped others work through complicated situations that were beyond the ability of most to resolve. He'd drive up in a sleek car. He wore a classy suit and tie and carried a leather briefcase. He looked smart and successful.

That impressed me, since I was usually wearing sweat-stained overalls and dirty boots that reeked of hog bleep. I was in my mid-teens when I watched Jim confidently stroll up to the farmhouse, and I stopped him to ask a question.

"What is it you do again?"

As he kindly explained his work to me, a bond was born. Jim and his CPA partners became mentors and advisors to me for decades after that because I realized we spoke the same language. That's *mathematically*-speaking.

You see, I struggled in school when it came to English literature. When my professors asked me to read Shakespeare or *The Canterbury Tales*, they might as well have been asking me to translate Swahili or Navajo.

I failed the English 220 test three times. My girlfriend and future wife, who always earned higher marks than me, offered a friendly suggestion after the third flop: "Maybe you should actually *read* the books."

Yeah, I was a CliffsNotes kind of guy back then. Always looking for the shortcut when it came to studying. If they'd had Google back then, I would have done much better.

At times, I never thought I'd make it past high school—if that far. I told my parents I wanted to quit school in grade ten and go into an auto mechanic apprentice program like my cousin. My dream was to work in my dad's Massey Ferguson garage. I loved being there, pumping gas and fixing tractors, cars, and tires. But my mother insisted that I stay in high school.

My grades suffered because I loved working in the garage so much more. It was more challenging to me! We were already the first generation of our agrarian family to go to high school, and my mom insisted that I finish it and then go on to be the first in the family to attend university. That was the only thing that kept me in school, along with my natural gift with numbers, which helped me find my niche in the world of accounting and business.

I mentioned earlier that my children call me "the human calculator," and they were not the first to make that observation. My teachers soon realized that while I'd never write the great American novel, I had a good shot at solving the Pythagorean theorem. (I know, that's geometry, but it's still in my wheelhouse.)

One of my problems with reading as a child was that my mind was always racing. I was never diagnosed with any type of attention deficit disorder, since nobody knew what that was back then, and I'm not sure that applies to me even now. But everyone who knows me will tell you that my mind works fast and my mouth struggles to keep up.

Although I certainly don't do it on purpose, I'm known to speak quickly, and people sometimes have trouble understanding me. I even had a friend who brought this up while "roasting" me at an event. He pulled out a translation gizmo that slowed down my speech to about half my normal speed. He claimed that was the only way he could comprehend what I was saying! Of course, the whole room was in stitches as they all felt the same way. I am trying harder these days to slow down!

NUMBERS NERD

Fortunately, I have never had to make a living as a public speaker, because my racing mind just so happens to love numbers and any calculations involving them. I solved math problems for fun as a kid, and in more recent years, I've become addicted to sudoku puzzles, which are logic-based brain games.

You are probably thinking, *Bob is a numbers nerd*, and you would be correct. I do not try to hide it. In fact, my affinity for numbers has proven to be beneficial in the business world. No surprise, then, that I followed our family CPA into accounting classes and a degree in economics in college.

I initially majored in marketing, but after flunking out of that field of study, I was "encouraged" to shift my major to economics and finance. There, I found my niche in accounting. I always tell college students to be patient and keep searching until they find a field that fits naturally for them and stirs their passion. As the old saying goes, "If you love your job, you will never have to work another day in your life!"

I may be okay with numbers, but overall, my grades in college were not all that great. Okay, they were terrible. I never had a B in school, but it wasn't because I got all A's. My grades were mostly in the C's and D's realm.

Still, I did not want to return to farming, so in my senior year, I pounded out hundreds of job applications and résumés on my rented carbon-ribbon typewriter. They didn't have good copy machines or computers back then, so I had to type every copy. I targeted every accounting firm within 100 miles.

There was another reason I was desperate for a job—the love of my life. Myrna owned my heart from the time I first saw her among the other kids in the Sunday school class taught by my mother.

Unlike me, she found a job right after she graduated from nursing school at Toronto General Hospital. She'd worked as a nurse's aide at my family's nursing retirement center since she was seventeen years old, so she already had a lot of experience in the field.

After she graduated college as a registered nurse, she took a job at a large general hospital in London, Ontario, which felt like a big city to us at the time. After graduating in 1972, and a lot of begging, I managed to get hired as an intern in the same city by a small, three-partner accounting firm. I only stayed there for a few months.

Finally, another of my accounting firm applications paid off. I got a call, and later, a job offer, from the Waterloo office of the international accounting firm Peat Marwick Mitchell & Co., which, after a merger, became known as KPMG.

Shortly thereafter, Myrna also agreed to become director of my family's nursing center. I already was doing the accounting for the center, so we had many lessons to learn about working as a team. I prepared the payroll and kept track of finances per day, while she took great care of the patients.

Back then, you had to have three years' work experience as a public accountant before you could take the CPA exam, which involves several days of intense tests. There is a fifty-fifty pass-fail rate. Some people have to take it two or three times before passing. Others never make it.

By the time I took this all-important exam, I'd become much better at studying and preparation during three more years of taking university accounting and business credits, as well as participating in KPMG's in-house training program. I just had a natural affinity for the field of accounting, and I passed the exam on my first try! I had finally found my strength, and it felt great to put it to good use.

BREAKING AWAY

Accounting firms at the time, like Wall Street investment banks, were breeding grounds for entrepreneurs. Young employees often find that these types of employers are often highly structured, demand long hours, and don't pay all that much initially.

However, when you work in banking and accounting, you have access to many business situations. You figure out quite quickly what businesses generate serious cash and income, and you are also in a position to see new markets opening up.

I worked for the small public accounting firm for three months at $5,700 a year, and then moved to Peat Marwick (now KPMG), where I started at $6,600 a year and earned a quick promotion to $11,000, and then to $15,000 by the time I left.

However, by this point, I was hungry for something more, like the really big money the partners were earning for doing the heavy lifting for clients. I wanted to reap more of the benefits of my own work, so I departed and joined forces with another CPA my age to start our own accounting firm, Schlegel & Moore.

When I gave notice that I would be leaving KPMG, I thought my boss would be happy for me. Instead, he was concerned and asked that I leave right away. It surprised me to be treated like that, and I vowed to always be kind to my good employees if they ever wanted to make a change.

One of my favorite clients had actually suggested I start my own firm, and helped to make it one of the fastest growing independent accounting firms in town. They had promised to switch their business to mine, and I think that qualified them as another blessing from an angel in my life.

The client that encouraged me to strike out on my own was a family-owned lumber company in St. Jacobs, a pretty little community just a few miles north of Waterloo. The owners were clients who became friends, but of course, I think they were also looking to save a few bucks on their accounting bills by switching over to my smaller firm.

I'd actually thought about getting into the lumber business, too, but my new firm grew quickly, and between that and helping with the nursing retirement center financials, I kept very busy. Then, a former senior partner I had worked with at KPMG joined our firm after a year or so, and he brought a bunch of great clients along with him.

My entrepreneurial drive was kicking into gear more and more. I'd been helping out my parents by handling the books for their nursing care facility, since I knew they'd be looking to retire one day. Myrna had also been working with them, full time, pretty much managing all of the medical aspects, as well as human resources and staff training.

So, slowly, we were drawn into that business, which was also very service-oriented. I even became president of the Ontario Nursing Home Association at one point. I was wearing many hats and Myrna was even busier than me, but we both realized that Canada's system of socialized medicine was changing and making the nursing center business more difficult to grow.

We had heard that there were better growth opportunities in that business across the border to the south. To find out for ourselves, we made several trips to Sun Belt states, searching California, Arizona, Texas, and Florida, talking to real estate agents and business brokers.

Texas seemed the most promising after we investigated a bit. It did not have socialized medicine like Canada, and was instead private pay. We realized we could provide luxury facilities with set charges at market rates. We also liked that Texas had right-to-work labor laws, which helped improve our chances for success.

You see, Myrna and I do not feel that unions belong in a healthcare setting. As we have experienced with Covid-19, unions will sometimes get their staff to walk off the job, and this is certainly not conducive to the care that our residences would require.

Here's what I believe you need in order to succeed. Treat your staff well. Listen to their needs and requests. Provide good working conditions. Pay them well. And always work as a team. Then both staff and managers will flourish. None of our centers in Canada or the U.S. ever were unionized.

We had previously been through a nasty union vote in our family-owned center, which we won. The employees rejected the union, which had been trying for years to unionize them. It was a difficult time for us because longtime employees did not want the union, but some of our newer employees did. It put a strain on many friendships.

So, we looked to Texas, where the big question was this: Could a couple of Canadian country kids make it in the land of oil tycoons and Dallas Cowboys?

Yes!

The only slightly smaller question was: Just how long a biweekly commute was it from Ontario to Texas, with two or three or four kids in the car?

Endless! (Actually, we came to enjoy these trips, believe it or not!)

Chapter Two

PEP: PERSISTENCE, EDUCATION, ENTREPRENEURSHIP, AND PASSION

Before we delve into the nuts and bolts of starting, growing, and running your own business, I want to help you first build a foundation for the most important factor to ensure a successful entrepreneurial career.

That would be *you*.

Your success depends on your levels of persistence, your pursuit of lifelong education, your entrepreneurial drive, and your passion for business opportunities. I'd also add that the quality of your partnerships, in business and in life, is equally important. This all adds up to an exciting purpose that inspires you to jump out of bed every morning.

I call my approach to entrepreneurship "PEP" to reflect those critical factors for success. These are the foundational pillars for a successful life as an entrepreneur. Before you make your first sale or seal your first deal, you should give some thought to each of these factors, because they will determine not only the level of success you achieve, but also the quality of your life.

To make sure you start off on the right path, let's take a look at each of these critical considerations:

Persistence: This is the most essential element of all because you will encounter many challenges as an entrepreneur, but if you refuse to give up, you will find success.

Education: While a basic education and even advanced college degrees are required in many fields, I believe self-education throughout your lifetime is an important factor in anyone's success. The pursuit of knowledge of markets, producers, and distributors are essential for entrepreneurs because that is how you find new opportunities as you pursue financial and career success. There are lessons everywhere in every experience that you have, and you should strive to learn and grow as much as you can from these experiences.

Entrepreneurship: Entrepreneurship is your path to self-determination and the driving purpose of your life. It is not a job, it is a calling, and your path to success is shaped by your values and principles. As a successful entrepreneur, you have the opportunity to create jobs that support your family and your community.

Passion: You have to be driven by a high level of passion for whatever you pursue because you will encounter many challenges and frustrations along the way. So, I'll say it again, "You must love your job and what you do!"

Partnerships: To have a truly fulfilling life, you must build strong and mutually rewarding relationships with your spouse, family members, friends, employees, customers, suppliers, and other stakeholders, because your business is not just a job—it's your life.

PERSISTENCE

My friend Byron Roth, chairman and CEO of Roth Capital Partners, is another "numbers guy" and entrepreneur who grew up in a small Mennonite farm community in Iowa.

Byron told me that he learned persistence from his older brother when they played basketball as kids.

"We played pickup games against each other. Even though I was younger, I was a better player and I usually won, but he would never let me quit for the day until he'd won a game.

"He'd say, 'Let's play one more; this time I'm gonna cream you.' He started every game feeling confident. He always kept hustling, doing his best. He could lose nineteen straight games to me, but he wouldn't quit until he could finally walk away a winner.

"His attitude was, 'It's not over until I win or reach my goal or dream.' And I have to say, that attitude served him and others in business very well, including you, Bob."

Why is it important that you be persistent as an entrepreneur? Because there is rarely an easy path to success. You will encounter many roadblocks and obstacles, but if you refuse to give up, you will find a way. Unlike sports, in business, there does not have to a loser. The best solution is always a win-win!

At Pavestone, we had a sales manager who was persistent and highly motivated, but Myrna managed to supercharge his enthusiasm. We were at a company celebration with him when he declared that he wanted to go after Walmart as a customer. This was fairly early in Pavestone's history, when we were still selling mostly to contractors and landscape businesses. We didn't think Walmart, the largest big-box retailer in the world, was within our reach.

But when this sales manager suggested going after their business, my wife said, "If you get Walmart's business, we will buy you a Mercedes!"

It took a while, but five years later, we bought him the Mercedes. Now, that's a way to encourage persistence! Being an entrepreneur isn't a job. It's a lifestyle built around your businesses. You have to be all in, fully engaged, and willing to do whatever it takes to make your business successful.

Now, that doesn't mean you have to ignore your family or neglect your relationships. In fact, Myrna and I always took our kids along for the ride, quite literally! In 1978, we decided to grow our nursing retirement center business by expanding into the United States. We had several reasons for doing this that I will speak about in the chapter on growing your business.

We had both worked in our family-owned nursing and retirement center, so we knew the business. So, we sold our house and used the profits as a down payment on a sixty-bed nursing facility in Stratford, Ontario, and we looked to expand.

We thought there would be more opportunities for growth in the United States. The initial investment to get in was more reasonable in Texas because it was one-third the cost of a Canadian facility, due to the private market competitive licensing laws, versus restricted licenses by the government.

Our plan was to buy underperforming properties and transform them into the prettiest, most comfortable, and well-operated nursing retirement centers in the community. We scouted several southern states before diving in with our first purchases in a North Dallas suburb.

We actually bought two facilities initially. A construction company built them. The facilities were very nice and of high quality, but building contractors were trying to run the nursing retirement centers, which wasn't working out. They didn't have experience in that field, so their management system wasn't up to the task, either.

Both of the centers were having trouble with state regulators and customer complaints. The operators wanted out. We saw this as a perfect test for our plan.

This was a great opportunity to see if we could expand into the United States. Canada's healthcare system worked on a single-payer reimbursement program for these centers, and the staff was mostly unionized. We saw more potential in Texas, where we felt non-union centers could give more compassionate care at private market rates.

We had moved into a rental home in Canada. I was twenty-nine. Myrna was twenty-seven. We'd never operated under U.S. rules and regulations, so we gave ourselves a few years to see how it went before we actually moved to the Lone Star State. We were cautious, signing just a six-month lease on our first Dallas apartment. (We ended up renewing that lease six times!)

I clearly remember going with Myrna to Target in Dallas to buy place settings and cutlery. We also rented a very inexpensive sofa and chair, a TV, and a card table. We didn't want anything fancy because we were not sure how long we would be there. We were not about to spend any money we didn't need to spend until we got a better grip on whether our plans in Texas would succeed.

We also wanted to make sure the expansion into the U.S. would work before moving the family. So, we began commuting more than 1,100 miles one-way, every few weeks, with our two very young kids, often with my mother, a nanny, and Axel, our dog. How is that for persistence and PEP?

To save money and time, we made the drive with as few stops as possible. Our Canada-to-Texas commute usually took around twenty-two hours depending on traffic and pit stops. We told people it was simple: Go to Nashville and turn right.

We made the regular commute from 1979 until 1985, when we finally moved to Dallas. In the later years, we flew more often, but Myrna and I and the kids actually have fond memories of those long drives, even if there were times when we wanted to just pull over and sleep for a day.

Our two oldest kids, Kimberly and Kirby, remember riding in the back of the van with their grandmother, the nanny, and Axel, while playing games and singing along to tapes from Sesame Street and Raffi—who was their favorite entertainer back then.

This was before mandatory car seats, so Kirby and Kim would take turns serving as "navigator" and singing to keep whoever was driving awake. While one kept the driver entertained, the other would sleep in the back of the van. We rarely stopped, except for gas, food, and to empty out the kids' potty chairs.

Making that drive was a grind physically, but we had a plan and a passion for providing a high level of care, along with a high standard of living for our residents. The passion for growing this business kept us on the path.

My friend Jeff Rich, former CEO of a Fortune 500 company, and another avid businessman with diverse holdings, says he sees those long, family drives between our homes in Canada and Texas with the kids, dog, nannies, grandparents, and sometimes aunts and uncles as "an important foundational story."

"You and I met in the Young Presidents Organization [YPO] where you were a mentor and role model for my generation. We were all successful in business at that point, but many struggled with their personal relationships because they were so driven in their careers," Jeff says. "YPO stressed finding a balance between business and family. You didn't just talk about it, you lived it. You didn't play golf or have hobbies. Instead, you were devoted to your businesses and your wife and kids. So, for us, you were living proof that we could have great business careers and great family lives. We've watched all of your efforts bear fruit over the years as your kids are all successful in their own careers and they remain a very loyal and close-knit group."

Of course, there were tears from my wife at times when she was living out of a suitcase and going back and forth to Texas. I remember a night when she said, "Why can't we just go back to owning our own home with sheers in the bay window? I so often want to be like my friends and have a normal home."

I assured her that one day all this hard work would pay off! I think those trips really set the bar for Myrna and me, and they brought us closer together with our kids. We'd given up a comfortable home and an easy family life. There were a lot of sacrifices to be made. We didn't know at the time whether our nursing retirement centers in Texas would work out or not. There were a few scary moments.

Early on, we had major challenges from the state agency that regulates this type of business in Texas because of problems we inherited when we bought that first center. The state briefly shut our cash flow down with a "vendor hold" as we scrambled to come into full compliance, not even giving us a moment to improve the care in the facility.

There is a theory, as discussed in Malcolm Gladwell's *Outliers: The Story of Success*, that you really don't know what you are doing in any business until you've put in at least 10,000 hours training. Even at our young ages, Myrna and I had spent more than that amount of time caring for elderly residents. We had also both worked in care centers since we were teenagers. Myrna had worked in a nursing home through high school, and then she'd worked in similar care facilities as a registered nurse, so she'd seen just about everything.

I take that back. The one thing she had not ever seen in our Canadian properties was a cockroach. During our first week of operation in Texas, the health department found several during an inspection. They brought them to my wife and put a scare in her.

"What is *that?*" she said in horror.

The inspectors couldn't believe she'd never seen a cockroach, but that was the truth. They do exist in Canada, but Myrna had never run into one. Maybe they were just bigger in Texas and easier to spot. At any rate, she was horrified when presented with the creepy-crawly evidence.

We all cleaned up the place, and within several months, we were providing a much higher level of care and cleanliness and surpassing our residents' expectations.

Only our passion and experiences in our Canadian businesses kept us going when the state was cutting our cash flow down, the kids were crying in the van, the dog was barking, and we both wanted to run off and hide.

That is why you make sure you refuse to give up and keep at it! Myrna and I were still in our twenties, but we never could have pulled off this major move without that shared determination and dedication for starting and growing this business.

You, too, will need the extra energy, patience, and persistence to keep you on the path to success with your business because you will have to put in long hours and go the extra mile, or two, or thousand.

PRINCIPLES, VALUES, AND THE PURSUIT OF EDUCATION AND ENTREPRENEURIAL PURPOSE

While getting a good education, a college degree, and even an advanced degree are essential in many fields these days, I encourage all aspiring entrepreneurs to never stop expanding their knowledge, staying on top of technological developments, and remaining curious about the world around them.

Hunger for knowledge is a hallmark of all the best entrepreneurs I know. When they meet someone for the first time, especially those who share an entrepreneurial passion, they want to know all about them and their endeavors and their vision for the future. That is how we find opportunities to create new businesses.

Before you buy or start your own business, I also encourage you to sit down and think about the values that are important to you. These are the standards that you live by or aspire to live by in your daily life. Honesty is one example of a value we should all try to uphold in our lives. Perseverance is another one.

Your principles are the rules and beliefs that govern your actions, and they are based on your values. Your business also reflects your principles and values, and it will not succeed if it does not include serving the needs of your customers.

Customers decide which businesses succeed or fail by voting with their wallets for those that look after their needs. Certainly, there are some business owners who have succeeded using predatory and cutthroat practices. But not many!

Questions you may want to consider: "How do you want to live your life? Do you want to spend it preying on your customers and fending off lawsuits and charges? Or do you want to be someone who is known for honesty, integrity, and fairness in their dealings?"

I encourage you to run your business according to the highest values and principles you can identify, so that at the end of your run, you can be proud of your accomplishments and the trusting relationships you've built. Remember: You choose how you want to live and who you want to associate with.

I've known entrepreneurs and business owners at both ends of this spectrum. I prefer to stand on the side of those who do the right thing, even if occasionally they don't make as big a profit as they'd like—or any at all on a certain project!

I've even fallen prey to those at the other end of the spectrum from time to time, however. Most of them pay a steep price when the law catches up to them, or they go down in flames because of their reputation. Some smooth operators are very good at winning trust and then betraying it.

Like many entrepreneurs, I've learned the hard way that if a deal looks too good to be true, it often is. After we'd become established in Dallas and made friends with other entrepreneurs, Myrna and I hosted a party for a friend, where we met a high-profile guy who said he had a great deal for me.

This entrepreneur was a well-known multimillionaire whose company did billions in annual sales. The company's name was on buildings all over Dallas. And he'd been invited to a party thrown for a very good friend of mine. So, my defenses were down.

When he learned I was a native of Canada, he told me that he owned an aviation business there, a corporate aircraft brokerage. He had several jets that he'd purchased from the military. He intended to turn them into corporate executive jets, and offered to sell some to me at a great price—or at least what I *thought* at the time was a great price.

"You can get them refurbished and sell them for a big profit," he said. "I just don't have the time to do it."

I had owned a couple of different company jets for several years at this point, and had some experience at refurbishing planes.

He was a good salesman. I figured I could trust a guy who was so well known. I had friends who worked for him, and we also had many mutual friends.

I jumped on the deal without doing enough due diligence on the guy, or the jets. I purchased three jets with financing, expecting to flip them in twelve to eighteen months.

This turned out to be one of the worst deals I ever made— even worse than Car Bars—and the guy I bought the planes from proved to be one of the most unprincipled people I've ever met. He had no scruples at all. But in the end, I had only myself to blame, because I should have done more due diligence before buying those three planes.

We received only one jet in the first five years out of this "quick" three-jet deal. The other two were never certified air-worthy to fly, and after ten years, we still hadn't taken delivery of the third one! During this time, I went to the guy who sold them to me and said, "If I was a car dealer and sold you a car that I could not ever deliver, I'd return your money. So, I'd like my money back for the jets that you could not deliver."

"I'm not as nice a guy as you are, Bob" he said.

Despite our best efforts to work it out, we were forced to sue him. Of course, he fought us.

This was a costly lesson in terms of both money and time, but I learned a lot about what it is like to deal with an unscrupulous character, and I reaffirmed that I never want to be that sort of person. I also never wanted to be in a business that put my personal reputation in danger.

There are many gray-area businesses out there that might tempt you with promises of low up-front costs, big returns, and minimal effort, but you have to ask yourself whether it is worth damaging your reputation and your relationships. You have to trust your gut. If you get involved with a business that just doesn't feel right for you, it probably isn't.

Several times, I've gotten really excited about an investment opportunity, but they've wanted to close in just a few days or some other tight time frame. Experience has taught me that it's not a good idea to rush into any deal. You need to take time to research the business and its market properly. A quick deal for the seller may not be a good deal for the buyer. Due diligence is extremely important.

TAKE THE LONG-TERM VIEW

I've known entrepreneurs who've jumped on new business opportunities without giving enough thought to the nature of the path they are taking. There are many lucrative businesses that prey on customers who are unsophisticated and naïve. Some sell the modern-day equivalent of snake oil.

Once you invest in these sordid ventures, there is often no turning back without severe penalties. And if you stick with it, you can lose the trust and respect of those who matter most to you, and perhaps worse, you can also lose respect for yourself.

Don't let that happen to you. Take the time and make the effort to find a business that you are proud to be part of, one that sells top-quality products or services and fosters loyalty and gratitude from your customers and clients.

An example of a guiding principle or mission statement for a business and its leader might be something like this: *Our purpose is to profit and grow by serving the needs of our customers and exceeding their expectations with integrity and the highest quality products and services in our industry.*

Certainly, every business owner sets out to make a profit and keep growing the business, but by taking it a step further and defining *how* you plan to do that is critical not only for you as the business leader, but also for your employees, suppliers, and customers.

When you create a statement of purpose for your business, you are saying up-front to everyone involved that you are focused on serving others, not on taking advantage of them or trying to squeeze every dime out of them. You want to win their loyalty and respect, as well as their business.

Here is another benefit: When your business is in alignment with your values, principles, and purpose, then passion for your work will flow naturally because you will take pride in the products and services you provide to your customers. You will love going to work each day!

MAKE A STATEMENT TO LIVE BY

When I start a new business, I create a company mission statement to give all stakeholders, employees, suppliers, and customers so they know what the business stands for, what I stand for, and what I expect of our people. For my most recent start-up, Bedrock Logistics, the values we embrace are listed on our website and in company materials given to each employee.

Our values are:

Integrity: We manage high-level business challenges without sacrificing our belief in doing the right thing.

Commitment: We strive for long-term business partnerships that go beyond serving our customers.

Mission: Our goal is to make dependable logistics easily attainable for our customers.

Vision: We aim to provide a technology-driven logistics service delivered with excellence, integrity, and commitment.

Excellence: We will push every aspect of our company to the limit to provide our customers with the ultimate transportation experience.

Your values and principles can serve as guideposts for you and your employees. We make sure everyone on our team knows our values and our purpose statement. We remind them regularly of their importance, and we tell them that if they ever have any questions or doubts, to review them before taking any action that might conflict with them.

CORE VALUES AND CORNERSTONES

There are no set rules for how to present your guiding values and purpose. I've seen other companies list their beliefs and provide a mission statement. The important thing is to give serious thought to aligning your company with your standards early in the process, and then following through by training your employees to incorporate them into everything they do. It's important to involve employees in creating and evaluating your purpose so they all will buy into it.

Your customers and clients shouldn't have to ask what your company stands for. They should experience it in every dealing, with every employee.

My son-in-law Troy is partner in a company, and has established three cornerstones that it posts on its website and in its marketing materials: Consistent Quality, Superior Service, and Integrity. The company statement also says that to protect its exceptional reputation, they have established 5 Core Values that form the foundation for its performance and conduct each day:

"Our Core Values clarify who we are and what we stand for. They guide our business relationships and practices, our decision-making, and our training, coaching, and counseling. They represent what drives our organization and apply to our interaction with fellow employees, customers, suppliers, and the general public. Our entire team works hard with the direction of our management framework to learn and grow every day."

Those Core Values are:

1. We build TRUST—Trust is a combination of our team's ability to demonstrate integrity and reliability in everything we do.

2. We work hard to be the BEST—Our team's commitment and dedication comes from highly motivated individuals who take their jobs seriously.

3. We find SOLUTIONS—Our team is empowered to see opportunity in every challenge—we find a way to get YES!

4. We RESPECT each other—We listen and offer encouragement to help achieve common goals.

5. And most importantly—We have FUN!

STAYING ON TRACK

Troy and his business partner have revised this statement of values from time to time to make sure it stays up to date. After launching a start-up company, you may want to take a look at your values and purpose statement after a year of operation and determine whether any adjustments need to be made. It is not unusual, after all, for any new company to make major changes in its products or services after testing the marketplace, or when the economy shifts.

Our philosophy is a revised version of "If at first you don't succeed." Our version is "Try it. Fix it? Try it. Fix it."

After the start-up period shifts into a growth period, it's generally unwise to make any changes in your values and purpose statements without careful consideration about the impact it might have on your employees and customers.

It's much easier to create a list of values and a statement of purpose than to live by them, especially when the economy is tanking, your market is evaporating, and the competition is threatening to stomp you into the ground. But that is precisely when you need them the most.

Without a doubt, there will be times when you may be tempted to stray from your values or from your mission, but if you put in the time at the beginning to decide what really matters to you in the long view, the correct path should be clear.

Taking the long view is another important part of creating your guiding values and purpose statements. Most entrepreneurs go into businesses that they intend to run for many years before either selling them or handing them over to family members or trusted partners.

Here are a few long-term questions that I suggest you consider as you begin any business:

- *What do I want to achieve as my end goal?* You can leave this open or closed, but it is always there and you'll want to change as circumstances and opportunities shift. Other variations on this question might include: *Is this a business I want to grow and leave to my children and grandchildren? Is this a business I want to grow and then sell after a certain point? If so, what is my time frame?*

- *How do I want my customers and employees to feel about this company at the end of the day?*

- *How do I want this business to impact the community over the long term?*

- *How do I want my spouse and our children to feel about this business over time?*

PASSION

You may have read articles or books advising you to build a business around something you have a passion for. That's usually interpreted to mean finding ways to profit from a hobby or a talent. Examples of this might be the car enthusiast who starts his own sports car dealership, the musician who opens her own recording studio, or the computer geek who creates apps and software programs.

Each of our grown kids have built businesses around their interests. Our son followed his passion for sports into minor league hockey and baseball teams, and a sports agency representing athletes. Our three daughters have each founded companies based on their passions for fashion and lifestyle blogging, writing books, children's clothing, retail marketing, and real estate.

There is a lot to be said for turning a hobby or a talent into a money-making venture. I highly recommend it. But don't rule out other opportunities. I know many entrepreneurs who are simply passionate about the process of finding opportunities to create and grow businesses of all kinds.

Like many of my entrepreneurial friends, my passion isn't focused on one field of business or any particular product. We're like gardeners who enjoy planting, nurturing, and growing things, whether they are flowers, herbs, vegetables, or exotic grasses—or a paver manufacturing company.

My two biggest business successes so far have been our chain of PeopleCare Heritage Centers and a paving stone manufacturing company. Now, my parents moved off the farm to run a similar nursing retirement facility when I was a teenager, but I certainly didn't grow up yearning to run a chain of them. And while I like nice landscaping, paving stones weren't exactly the stuff of my childhood dreams, either.

Yet I truly enjoyed the many years I was involved in both businesses because we were able to build successful companies that provided top-notch services and goods to appreciative clients and customers. In the process, we created thousands of jobs that had a positive impact on the lives of our employees and our community, as well as all our suppliers' companies and the families they supported.

When we sold those businesses, our efforts paid off and gave us the opportunity to fulfill a greater purpose, which included building security for our children and grandchildren, and making a positive difference in the lives and careers of our employees, associates, and others through philanthropy.

Another key to firing up your passions is to get into a business that engages you on multiple levels, plays to your strengths, challenges your mind, and builds upon your talents and abilities. And last but not least, it should help you build more resources than you ever could working for someone else!

As an analytical, math-minded guy, I especially enjoy homing in on the financial aspects of my business and figuring out ways to improve performance. I really get engaged in solving problems and puzzles. When I'm locked in on a set of spreadsheets, I lose track of time. I get so focused, I don't hear any background noise.

I love that feeling of being in the flow of my business. When you can become that engrossed in what you do for a living, it's a very good indicator that you are in the right line of work.

None of my past companies will ever make the list of "Top Ten Most Exciting & Sexy Businesses." I get that. But when I look back at how grateful our nursing retirement center residents and their families were for the high quality of care we provided and the life-enrichment programs we offered, I find that pretty darn exciting.

One of my current businesses is Bedrock Logistics, a start-up that was later a spin-off from Pavestone Co., which I sold in 2012 after building it from the ground up over thirty-two years. At Pavestone, we developed our own transportation fleet and efficient delivery systems because handling such heavy, low-price-per-ton concrete products takes some special expertise and equipment.

When I sold Pavestone to Quikrete, the new owners had their own transportation fleet, which was fine with me because I had a plan for this spin-off. My goal is to make it the Uber of the trucking transport industry, the bridge between companies trying to deliver goods and truckers looking for loads. Our goal is to provide the most efficient way to match them up with the latest technology.

As with Uber, one of the major components to this logistics-based business is cutting-edge software customized for our purpose. Logistics is a numbers game, so this business really does play to my passion and my strengths, perhaps more than any other I've owned. My big hairy audacious (BHAG) goal is to up this game from a $50 million business into a $500 million business in the next few years!

A PASSION FOR THE PROCESS

A passion for the process of creating and running a business is what drives many entrepreneurs to have diverse companies across various categories and fields. I thought of this while advising my son-in-law Troy when he was looking to start another business of his own.

Troy, who is married to my daughter Kari, had worked for seventeen years as a sales executive in the hair care industry with Paul Mitchell Systems, but he has always had an entrepreneurial spirit. Even while working there, he started an offshoot business, Dollar Camp, that provided financial responsibility training for hairstylists.

Troy, a native of Iowa, was a quarterback for the University of Nebraska, and I'm fairly certain he never dreamed that he'd start a hair-care related business. He and a partner saw that there was a need for personal and business financial training in their industry, however, and they jumped on the opportunity to provide it.

I never said anything to Troy about this, but I could tell that one day he would want to break out of the corporate salary world and run his own business full time. As an athlete and natural leader, he has a strong competitive spirit. He gets fired up by competing to be the best in whatever he does.

He also has strong entrepreneurial instincts. Just a couple years ago, Troy founded another company spun off from his love of hunting. He came up with the idea for this business while discussing the fact that the deer and other wild game he and his brothers hunted would often flee if they picked up the scent of humans.

The brothers believed there was likely a strong market among hunters for products that would effectively counter the finely tuned noses of their prey. They took that idea and ran with it, developing an entire line of products called Scent Kapture, which has already found a receptive market.

As I was beginning this book, my son-in-law decided to make the leap as a full-time entrepreneur. This time, he partnered with a gentleman I'd been mentoring for fifteen years in business. He had contracted with the company to make cleaning chemicals and his Scent Kapture hunting product. Then they found an opportunity to take over a bankrupt operation that could increase their capacity at least tenfold. They bought this ninety-five-year-old business because they felt it had considerable growth potential.

They began manufacturing and packaging a wide range of cleaning and maintenance products, including hand sanitizers and disinfectants. In the past, the business struggled under the third generation of family ownership. A private equity company had tried to turn it around, but failed. Troy and his partner brought in new people and rejuvenated sales.

I've helped Troy with financial advice and made suggestions for other changes. Once again, his passion for this company isn't so much about its products. He simply enjoys the game of taking a business to a higher level and building something of even greater value.

Troy says he is still in the "liquids" business, after more than ten thousand hours of experience at Paul Mitchell. He has simply shifted from the liquids used in hair care products to those in soaps and cleaning products. His goal is to help create a cleaner environment by using environmentally-friendly processes and creating "green" products.

So, keep in mind that you can find *passion* in many ways as an entrepreneur. Some businesses offer more day-to-day excitement than others. Some are more fun to talk about with friends. Some demand more creativity. But even paving stones and nursing retirement centers, or logistics and real estate, can make for very interesting lines of work and rewarding lives.

I really can't stress enough that as an entrepreneur, you aren't just starting a business, you are embracing a lifestyle. Your success as an entrepreneur and as a person will depend in large part on the quality of the relationships you build. Everyone who is in any way involved or affected by your business is, in effect, a partner and stakeholder in it. Those critical relationships include your employees, customers, suppliers, and even your competitors, to some degree.

I know that may seem like a strange concept, that your competition is your partner, but I'm here to tell you that when the largest business I'd ever built went through an incredibly difficult period, my competitor—the largest in our market—turned out to be not just a partner, but an angel.

YOUR COMPETITOR AS A MEASURING STICK

I have a policy that runs counter to the intensely competitive world of business today. I take my highest-quality competitor to lunch every few years. Just because you are in competition doesn't mean you have to be enemies. I made that suggestion recently at a big meeting of young business executives and it caused quite a stir.

One person declared me "the smartest guy in the room," but others weren't so sure. Many entrepreneurs simply want to crush their competition, not break bread with it.

Some even interpreted that statement to be a kinder take on the old adage, "Keep your friends close and your enemies closer." But again, that's not the approach I advocate. Nor do I suggest you meet with your competition once a year so you can somehow gain an edge, or wine and dine them with fake news.

I am a competitive person, don't get me wrong. I wake up every morning with my mind buzzing about ways to gain a competitive edge. But I also believe there is more to be gained by seeing that you and your business rivals have a lot of processes in common.

After all, most industries have trade associations that work to improve the playing field, from government relations, raw materials, sourcing and staff training, technical product support, quality standards, and customer reviews and national advertising. So it makes sense that you may have common interests to discuss for the benefit of both companies.

Now, you are still competitors, of course, and you have to be careful. You may run into cutthroat individuals who have scarcity mentalities and want your company to shrivel up and die so they can dominate the market. I probably wouldn't suggest you take that type of competitor to dinner, obviously.

But I have found that I often have more in common with my competitors than I do with most other people. We are in the same business, after all. Most business owners are simply trying to hang on to and grow their market share without malice toward their competition.

Your industry colleagues usually have had the same problems as you and are happy to share things that worked for them! And whether you like them or not, your competition is a partner in the sense that they drive you to work harder, think smarter, and stay on top of market shifts.

In the small farming community where I grew up, it wasn't unusual for competing businesses to help each other out from time to time. Farmers can be competitive with each other as far as who gets their crops planted and harvested first, and who has the highest yield or the best herd of cows, but they also work together and depend on each other in lean times.

It's always smart to know who you are competing against and to get a sense of their business philosophy, their view of the market, and their plans down the road. Also, it's a good way to help your kid find a first job, get some real-life experience working for someone else, and get their ten thousand hours before they work in the family business.

And then there is this: At some point, your competitor could turn out to be the "angel" who buys your business when you are ready to retire. Or you may want to buy the competitor's business one day. That has happened to me. In fact, my largest competitor did serve as my "angel" after Pavestone went through an incredibly difficult time.

I will describe that story in greater depth later in the book, but for now, just keep in mind that some of the most important relationships and partnerships you build in your entrepreneurial career might be with those competing for your customers and clients.

SERVING YOUR CUSTOMERS

Walmart founder Sam Walton said: "There is only one boss. The customer. And he can fire everybody in the company from the chairman on down, simply by spending his money somewhere else."

Most entrepreneurs understand that customer service is essential to their long-term success. The problem is that we often get caught up in the drive to grow our businesses and focus on attracting new customers or increasing profits while dropping the ball on building and maintaining relationships with existing customers.

You can grow your business, attract new customers, and still serve your existing customers; it just takes discipline, focus, and personal attention. Maintaining personal relationships with each customer becomes more challenging as your business grows, of course, but that is why you hire more people and train them to follow the values you established for your company.

Our nursing retirement center staff included a former pastor who became our community relations counselor. He helped us create a life-enrichment program that emphasized to staff members the importance of respecting our guests and their privacy, supporting their independence as much as possible, creating a stimulating atmosphere, and providing a highly social environment.

Too many nursing retirement centers—and businesses in general—get caught up in creating rules and regulations that serve their own needs, instead of serving the needs of their customers and clients. For example, many such centers have strictly enforced visiting hours, which limit opportunities for family and friends to interact with loved ones.

Our facilities had a far more friends-and-family-friendly policy on visiting hours. It said: "Come as often as you can and stay as long as you like."

That open-door policy set a tone that said, "We are a community, and we care about each other." We backed that up by making it a policy to serve as problem solvers, facilitators, and supporters of our residents. We also gave our frontline staff members the flexibility to make decisions and resolve problems. Sometimes with elderly residents, the best response to a complaint is simply to listen while being respectful and compassionate. We always stressed the importance of maintaining long-term relationships in all of our businesses.

There can be some challenges when working with customers who are also friends who we would socialize with regularly. When I had my CPA firm, I found that clients who were also personal friends sometimes had problems with me asking them questions about their finances. I had to assure them that my professional ethics and personal integrity meant that I would never discuss their financial matters with others. I also had to be diplomatic, and always careful to protect their privacy.

MAINTAINING WORK-FAMILY BALANCE

Relationships with customers are critical, and so are those within your staff and family. You do not have to sacrifice your personal relationships in order to run your own business. You can and should do everything possible to have a well-rounded life. My own feeling on this is that you can't make it as an entrepreneur without the love and support of family, because there will be times when everything else falls apart.

Owning your own business is hopefully a way to make more money than you would working for someone else. My experience confirms that to be true, but there are certainly no guarantees. The rewards can be high, but so can the risks.

Just know that when you have "a job," it's what you do to make a living. But when you own a business, it's much more. There is no clocking out. You are always on call. Vacations will be difficult to schedule, if not impossible to take. And there really isn't an effective way to separate your work life from your family life. You can't quickly resign when things are bad one day and go work for someone else.

I've heard other entrepreneurs claim that they are able to compartmentalize their lives with work in one box and family life in another. Maybe some extremely disciplined people can pull that off, but I seriously doubt they can separate the two aspects of their lives for any long period of time.

Life just doesn't work that way. Business matters will interfere with family matters and vice versa. There is no way to perfectly balance the two. So why fight it? You have enough on your plate. However, be sure to set your priorities. I always had a rule that when my children called me at work, I took the call, even if I was in the middle of an important meeting.

The key is to always be aware that as an entrepreneur that you can't afford to neglect your business or your relationships. Be aware when the demands of work are limiting your time with those who are important to you, and do your best to communicate with them and find time to be with them. Let loved ones know that they are important to you, and also let your employees, customers, suppliers, and competitors know that you value your relationships with them, as well.

My friend Steve Durham, chairman of Americas Strategic Holdings, often teases me about my need to have my life, and everything in it, in alignment. When he visits our summer cottage on Lake Huron, Steve often pulls a prank on me that plays upon my need for symmetry.

He has observed that I am a little fanatic about making sure the beach and deck table chairs at the lake are spaced apart, angled equally parallel, and in a perfect symmetry for our guests. Now, the beach is just down from the cottage, but you can look out a window and see the row of deck chairs and it makes for a nice view.

But Steve knows that it drives me crazy if I look out and see the chairs are out of alignment. So, when he visits, my friend sneaks down there and moves the chairs around just enough to throw off the symmetry.

Then he goes back to the cottage and waits for my reaction when I look out and see they are out of whack. I've heard him laughing to himself as he watches me trek down there to restore order to my world.

Steve is a thoughtful guy, and he says my need to have the beach chairs lined up perfectly serves as a metaphor for the way I live and work.

"Even if I move the chairs just a few inches, you will spot the difference and go down there to put them back in place. You do the same in your life. You work hard to keep all parts of it in proper alignment," my friend notes.

"That is why you've been so successful in your businesses and in your relationships too. Whether it means driving from Canada to Texas with your family in the van all those years to get your nursing and retirement home business in the United States up and running, or letting your kids sit in on meetings, you will do whatever it takes to make sure all aspects are in balance and alignment, and that has worked out very well for you."

I'm not sure about all of that, but I guess Steve has a point. It takes a lot of effort, but you can have symmetry in your life, a good balance of work and family. If you are an entrepreneur and you have a family, you are in a family business, whether other family members work with you or not. You cannot separate these two critical parts of your life. Save yourself a ton of frustration and exhaustion and just accept the fact that you are all in this together, and then try to enjoy it.

We have always done that in our family, though I can't say it was a conscious decision in our early days. It just came naturally. We often discussed business in front of the kids, and sometimes that resulted in interesting feedback from them.

We all learned that there really was no way to separate work and family with two full-time entrepreneurs leading the household. On another occasion, Myrna had taken the kids to Wonderland, which was Canada's version of Disneyland, when I learned that one of our Texas centers was in upheaval.

A group of employees was pushing to unionize the staff. Another group was opposed. As owners, we felt we were paying a very good wage and we did not want a union stepping in to disrupt our operations. I felt bad when I went to pick up Myrna and the kids because they'd had such a great time and they were so excited.

I hated to rain on their parade, but I told Myrna what was going on and said, "You probably need to jump on a plane to Texas and get the staff settled down so they know all the facts before they vote on the union."

Myrna hopped on the next flight to Dallas in her shorts with no passport and no luggage. She arrived at midnight and went directly to the nursing retirement center to talk to her staff. She met with both sides all through the night and the next day. I do think she changed out of her shorts at some point, though! She finally convinced the staff to turn down the union after meeting with all three shift personnel.

She came home a few days later and said, "You know crisis management was not the sort of thing I ever thought I'd be doing."

We had a similar challenge in Canada with one of our centers there. Myrna got the call that some of our staff members who wanted to unionize had walked off the job. Myrna put on her RN uniform and took charge with the help of another nurse who stayed on. One of the staff members who wanted to unionize filed a complaint against Myrna for wearing nail polish, which is not allowed under the regulations. That's how silly it got to be.

Eventually, we had to go to the Labor Board and fight to keep the union votes on secret ballots so the happy employees felt secure in their decision.

Once again, Myrna found herself taking on multiple roles that were above and beyond the usual call of duty. But we made it work. You do whatever the job takes.

When Myrna was dealing with the unions in our first facility, she worked in whatever capacity she needed to get the job done, whether as a nurse or a nurse's aide. She always prided herself on the fact that there had never been a union in any of our businesses, even though others in our area were unionized.

Our employees never voted to unionize because we treated them well. They knew we wouldn't ask them to do anything that we wouldn't do ourselves. Myrna's nursing degree and my CPA certification were of enormous help in operating a nursing and retirement center.

Myrna and I have always worked as teammates with complementary skill sets, whether in business, or at home. Our friend Trisha Wilson says we must have taken the marriage guidance that says "two shall become one" seriously, because we became one heck of a team. That lifestyle was natural for us from the beginning of our marriage because we'd known each other since we were little kids.

My wife has a "whatever it takes" attitude, which proved to be invaluable when we entered the complex business of operating care centers for aging guests.

We had discovered early on that the state of Texas does not issue operating licenses to the owners of nursing retirement centers. It only issues those to certified administrators. We came to this realization when we bought a troubled facility and tried to fix it, but the administrator we'd inherited refused to make the changes we felt were needed.

She looked at us and saw a couple of kids—we were young, so she wasn't far off—and pulled out her ace card. She notified us, correctly, that the center's operating license from the state of Texas was in her name, not ours, so she didn't have to do what we told her.

Now, we could have fired her and hired another administrator, but we might have had the same problem. We realized we held the mortgage, but she held the license, which could have been a big problem.

Myrna had been a licensed administrator in Canada, but that license was not recognized as valid in Texas. The solution was for Myrna to go back to school for a semester, this time at the University of Texas in Austin, and get twelve extra credits to qualify her to be an administrator in Texas.

You can imagine the complications that caused for a young Canadian couple who was still driving back and forth to Texas with two very young kids. Myrna rented an apartment in Austin and went to class there during the week. She then came home to our apartment in Dallas on weekends and breaks, for one entire summer!

It is part of our family lore that, during that time, I potty-trained Kirby while also overseeing the finances of our nursing retirement operations. I'm sure Kirby thought I should have stuck to accounting.

That was a busy time for us, yet I could not resist jumping into another entrepreneurial opportunity. Just three months into our new venture in Texas, I was offered a chance to invest in a new paving stone manufacturing company of a Canadian friend, who while visiting us in Dallas, got the idea to expand in Texas. More on Pavestone later!

To say we had a lot on our plate would have been an understatement. We had a full banquet table, and we were juggling all of the dishes and glassware. Where would we have been without a passion for what we were doing? Or without each other?

When Myrna came home on weekends, she'd have to check in on how things were going at the nursing retirement centers while reconnecting with the kids and coaching me off the cliff. She made it home for Mother's Day only to learn that we were short of kitchen staff at a facility we had just taken over, so we both went in, with the kids, to serve dinner.

Once we were there and surveyed the situation, we realized that there weren't enough meals prepared on this special day to feed all of our residents and their guests. So I had to run out, grab a bunch of fast food, and buy paper plates so we could serve everyone dinner.

Myrna was becoming firm and fair, which is a necessity for any business owner. I admired her growing management skills, but still, now and then, when I saw her assert herself as a leader, I would think to myself: *What happened to that shy woman that I married?*

Fortunately, we were young, committed, and driven to achieve the American dream of controlling our own destinies as entrepreneurs. Myrna and I really had a remarkable partnership, which isn't to say we didn't have any arguments and moments of sheer panic over the years.

She would be the first to tell you that once we had four kids, with the oldest entering high school, she really yearned to devote more of her time to being a mom. "Something has to give," she said at that time.

We had two very management-intense companies, and we tried two or three times to hire a senior executive to run the nursing center operations and give Myrna more time to be with the kids, but we couldn't find someone to run it at the level she expected.

Basically, we couldn't find another Myrna. That's when we started talking about selling the nursing retirement centers, which took several years to bring about. Once we worked that out and turned a handsome profit, it created opportunities for us to do bigger and better things in business—and for our family.

ANOTHER INTERVENTION FROM AN ANGEL

As you might suspect, I've spent many hours talking to our elderly residents. Many speak about their careers and what they did for a living, but far more want to talk about their children and grandchildren and other people important to them.

As much as I love creating and building businesses, my life would be empty without the love of my family. This lesson, perhaps the most important I will share with you in this book, has been brought home to me time and time again.

We were still living mostly in Canada but traveling back and forth to Texas in the winter of 1983 when I had an experience that helped elucidate what was really important to me. I had to fly from Toronto for a closing on another residential care home in Houston, but there was another thing on my mind as I left the house for the 100-mile drive to the airport.

I turned to Myrna and said, "Whatever happens, hang in there. It will be okay." I was talking about our shared concern for my father, who was in the hospital after suffering a heart attack. I was very concerned about him and stopped for a visit on my way to the airport in Toronto.

He was not doing well, at all. I promised him I'd be back as soon as possible. Once I was back on the road to the airport, I was surprised by a winter blizzard. The highway was covered in ice.

I wasn't too worried, because my heavy Oldsmobile Toronado had front-wheel drive. But that did not protect me from the truck that came flying across the median while spinning out of control. It hit my car head-on.

The highway patrol found me unconscious, with the steering wheel still in my hands, but it was no longer attached to the steering column. My car was destroyed. In fact, when my brother-in-law Dale went to the tow yard to retrieve my belongings, the operator said, "I'm so sorry about your brother-in-law being killed."

From the damage to my big car, he couldn't imagine that anyone had survived the collision. My guardian angels were definitely at work again. I was hospitalized with a severe concussion and other injuries, but once again, I managed to escape death.

Around this time, Myrna also considered taking medication to help alleviate her stress, but ultimately chose not to. Her decision proved to be a blessing, as we later discovered she was pregnant with our daughter Kari. Had Myrna taken the medication, she or our baby could have suffered harmful side effects.

MY FATHER AND ROLE MODEL

Tragically, my father died while I was still in the hospital recovering from my car accident. My sister Mary Gingerich recalls this as "a very hard time" for us all.

"Our father had a heart attack October 31 and remained in the hospital until he died December 26," Mary recalled. "During that same time, Bob had his accident. While our father was dying, Bob was fighting for his life in and out of consciousness. It was a Christmas of very sad memories for us all."

I was thirty-three years old when my role model passed away. I still miss him dearly. He was my role model for a giving, caring, high-energy entrepreneur who was always giving to others and to his community. He and my mother were not wealthy, yet they took in refugees from Europe, single mothers, a couple with two kids, and anyone else they found to be in need.

"Our house was small, and always full of people, and very disorganized because my mother was always so busy doing things for us and for others," my sister Mary recalled. "But we always had food, and everyone was welcome."

I advise you and other entrepreneurs to always stay focused on building and nurturing relationships even as you build your businesses. I know all too well that the love of friends and family is what truly matters.

There is one more important aspect to keep in mind as you grow your family and your business over the years, and that is this: Make sure you take the time to celebrate your successes and to express your gratitude. If you involve your family in your businesses, they should share in the good times as well as the bad, right?

It was only fitting that we shared the joy when we sold the group of nursing centers. We had long talked about taking an extended family vacation to educate our children about life around the world. So, once we completed the sale, Myrna looked at me and said, "I'm ready to take that trip with the kids we used to talk about!"

My response was, "Okay, but you have to plan it!"

We ended up taking a series of extended trips, which allowed us to check back in on our remaining business operations and family matters. We did take a tutor on most of the trips so the kids could keep up on their schooling. On one leg of this world tour, we traveled for three months straight, with twenty-one checked suitcases between the seven of us. We had one laptop and one mobile satellite phone back then, so textbooks also were carried everywhere to help the kids keep up with their classes. To make sure they could return to their schools when we returned, we funded four scholarships to hold their places.

Some of our greatest memories are from those trips. Our lives were often so hectic with our businesses and their sports and other activities, but these trips gave us more time to relax, simply enjoy being together, and share new experiences and adventures without being heavily scheduled. The kids became even closer to each other and to us, and I can't express how grateful Myrna and I are that we took that time to celebrate our success with our children.

I encourage all entrepreneurs to do the same if possible, and to always be grateful for the gift of loved ones, which is the greatest gift of all.

Chapter Three

SHOULD YOU BUY OR BUILD YOUR FIRST BUSINESS?

When I speak to college business students and other aspiring entrepreneurs, they often ask whether it is better to start a business from scratch or buy an existing business.

Both! I say.

I've launched businesses both ways, and many ways in between, over the years. We built up our nursing retirement center business by purchasing existing homes, many of which were struggling, and upgrading them significantly. My accounting firm and the Pavestone business were built from the ground up.

Establishing the accounting firm with my partners wasn't a major undertaking, but it did force me to give up my salary and regular paychecks. Starting Pavestone company was much more complicated. Our first plant was only $200,000, but over the years we had to construct and staff manufacturing plants around the country. The newer super plants now cost between $7 million and $17 million, with the costs rising over time as we built bigger and better facilities with more automation and capacity.

You can imagine what a massive amount of work and financing went into each plant. Eventually, after some incredible challenges that I will write about later, and after thirty-two years, we sold Pavestone and I used the profits from that sale to quasi-retire and invest in other ventures.

I learned from the sale of the nursing centers and Pavestone that building your business to a "platform" level can be very lucrative, though it requires great time, effort, and resources. The idea is that your business becomes so well-established that large companies see that they could acquire it and create an entire new platform or revenue stream for their corporations without having to invest all the time and money and risk in into starting another one themselves.

The large leverage buyout companies are willing to pay top multiples for a well-constructed platform business that someone else has created with their blood, sweat, and tears over several years. There is a great deal of risk involved in this, of course.

I wasn't aware of this approach early on in my entrepreneurial career, but I saw that both our nursing centers and Pavestone were snapped up when the timing was right for both sides. We see this happen increasingly in today's business environment, where giants like Amazon, Google, Facebook, and Big Pharma eagerly buy up successful tech firms or new medications that complement or add value to their operations.

I keep that in mind as I work on the company that I spun off from Pavestone, Bedrock Logistics. My goal is to turn this enterprise into a platform that one day will create options to keep as a cash cow or hopefully accept large offers from bigger companies.

Maybe you are working at a company with a division that could be spun-off. Or you see a need within the company you work for that you could serve with a new business. Many major businesses and entrepreneurs have used the spin-move. PayPal was spun-off from eBay. Liberty Media sprang from AT&T. And Agilent Technologies, which does $4.5 billion in sales, was originally a division of Hewlett-Packard.

One of my former big customers, Home Depot, sold its industrial supply division to a group of private equity firms for $8.5 billion, and the resulting business, HD Supply, became a publicly traded firm on NASDAQ and now has 650 locations in North America. It grew so well that Home Depot actually bought it back recently.

Just keep in mind, there are bound to be some surprises with any new, slightly used, or spun-off enterprise. Our son, Kirby, has also had considerable experience buying existing businesses. As an entrepreneur in the field of sports, he owned and operated two minor league hockey teams, a NAHL team in Texas and an AHL team in Iowa.

The first, a NAHL Junior A hockey team in Dallas, won three consecutive national Junior A Championships for a three-peat in back-to-back to back in 2004, 2005, and 2006!

With success on the ice, but not so much in the business office, we learned that the "business" of hockey in the 2000s didn't work well south of Pennsylvania. This lesson came after we bought the Texas Tornado hockey team and set them free to play in a beautiful new arena in the North Dallas town of Frisco.

After winning big on the ice, but investing much more than we ever intended, we sold the franchise to another Canadian so he could have his "fun" as well! We now enjoy watching one of our Junior A graduates, Ben Bishop, playing for the Dallas Stars.

Kirby also led our investment in a minor league Triple-AAA baseball team, the Tacoma Rainers in Washington State. The Rainers were a turnaround opportunity that had struggled for years in a fifty-year-old ballpark. Our son helped engineer the municipal financing and construction of a $40 million renovation to the old ballpark, which created a very popular venue around America's favorite sport, supported by the MLB Seattle Mariners.

Buying this active business was easier than starting from scratch because the team already had a venue and a fan base, and minor league baseball is a great business model. Even so, many changes were required to bring the team to a profitable position. Kirby accomplished that, and he actually had a lot of fun doing it!

The Rainers team was a profitable entity for him when he sold it. I know he misses being the owner, and he sometimes wondered if he did the right thing at the time. However, later I think he was relieved not to be the team owner when the Covid virus came and cancelled the entire season. If Kirby had still been the owner, he would have lost millions.

As we all can attest, there are pros and cons to consider in buying and selling a company. One may be better than the other for you, depending on your circumstances. The primary consideration is financial.

Do you have access to the funds you would need to start a business from a mere idea, and then keep it going and growing through the start-up phase? It is usually much cheaper to start your own business than to buy an existing one. It's also often the way new businesses get started (that is, of course, unless you can buy a struggling or bankrupt company).

Starting your own business from the ground up provides the opportunity to build it just the way you want it. You are free to choose the business name and location, and to build fresh relationships with financial institutions, suppliers, and customers.

However, starting from scratch also means you have to go through the laborious and costly process of building the business infrastructure, hiring and training your entire team, creating all of the essential processes for conducting transactions, maintaining inventory, finding suppliers, and developing your market.

In most cases, buying a small, existing business that's already profitable gets you rolling much faster and involves less overall risk than building your own company from the ground up. Often, it is easier to secure financing because the existing business already has positive cash flow and a product or service. Most come with quantifiable assets like a building, equipment, furnishings, inventory, and working capital, and, most importantly, customers!

There are also systems in place for operating the business, not to mention experienced employees to keep it running, and an established market or customer base.

Then again, there is always a reason the current owner is selling the business. Retirement or bigger opportunities can prompt a sale, but so can negative factors like a diminishing market or overwhelming competition, a disruptive technology, lawsuits, tax problems, or complaints about the quality of the product or service.

That's why it is so important to conduct a thorough due diligence investigation, so you know just what you are getting into before buying an existing business. Even then, you often can't detect problems with a business until you are there every day. And sometimes, there are major surprises awaiting new owners. We've had a number of those over the years.

KNOW WHAT YOU ARE GETTING INTO

Once we straightened out the problems with the first two nursing retirement centers we purchased in the Dallas area, state regulators were so impressed with our success at turning them around that they began calling us and suggesting other struggling centers we should try to manage or buy. This fit with our family heritage of trying to improve the lives of others by offering a high quality of care in high-end facilities with more amenities than our competitors. We added beautiful plush surroundings, chapels and ice cream parlors, limousine service, attractive facilities, and top-end dining menus long before our competitors followed suit.

After our first three years in Texas, we began buying or managing one center a year over the next thirteen years. We eventually had more than 2,200 beds and 2,500 employees in fifteen PeopleCare Heritage Centers, with two in Canada and the rest in the U.S.

Nearly all the facilities we purchased in Texas were available because they were in trouble with the state or with the banks that had made loans on them to the previous owners. We always spent a month or two investigating all aspects of the homes before we bought them. Because of her expertise in this field, Myrna did the medical due diligence and studied all the state inspection reports to see what we were getting into. She also conducted surveys of the staffs and the families of our residents.

Even then, we'd find problems that surfaced only after we'd made the deal and settled into daily operations. The fourth center we bought in the Dallas area had a particularly unique problem that we hadn't picked up on. It was housed in a modern, attractive, and very large building with two huge 140-bed wings that were sectioned off. One of the wings was shut down altogether. The other still had residents and was operating 140 beds with very few residents and very poor quality of care.

We also discovered that the closed wing had been taken over by illegal tenants after our initial inspection. That side was a racy horror movie waiting to happen. It had been shut down and abandoned by the operators, but mystery squatters had moved in, and they were operating a prostitution ring in what had become the X-rated wing.

One of the night staff members in the open wing was running the operation in the shuttered wing. The "customers" would climb into a window where the window air conditioner had been removed in the closed wing. A resident in the open wing who kept an eye on everything told me about it. "Check the wastebasket in the hallway," she said. "There are bad things going on over there."

So, we cleared out the illegal operation and secured that wing of the building to make sure they didn't come back.

There was another hint that this was to be our problem-child care home. After we signed the purchase papers, we came back to the facility to discover that someone had backed a pickup truck to the front door and stolen a beautiful grand piano from the lounge.

Myrna and I just looked at each other like, "What have we gotten ourselves into?"

We were buying existing centers with some sort of issue and bringing them up to the highest standards. Most of the time, we knew what we were getting into, but this was a peculiar situation. We leased it with the option to buy from the largest nursing retirement center chain in the country.

A few weeks later, I saw the president of that company at a conference, and he said, "I get on my hands and knees and pray every night that you will be able to turn that place around because we sure don't want it back!"

The situation with the sex workers on our property brings up a key reminder for every entrepreneur and aspiring entrepreneur. Always Inspect every new property thoroughly. You should never find yourself asking, "What have I gotten into here?" like I did.

But we put in many hours of hard work, sweat, and tears, and turned it around to the point that we had long waiting lists of people wanting to move in. My angel had done it again!

Whether starting your own business or buying an existing one, you should always practice due diligence. This is a big and important job, and many entrepreneurs hire due diligence companies that employ lawyers and accountants to do it for them because it is so time-consuming.

KEYS TO DOING DUE DILIGENCE

- ☐ Company and corporate records including Articles of Incorporation, bylaws, meeting minutes, organizational charts, shareholders and their holdings, list of states in which the company does business, annual reports for at least three years, list of all property owned and leased, all registrations, and company names.

- ☐ Public records including recorded liens, lawsuits, existing contracts, tax history, zoning compliance, safety or health violations, patent histories, advertisements, and news stories about the business.

- ☐ Any pending state and federal legislation that might impact the business negatively or positively, and the reputation of the business and its owner in the community and field of business.

- ☐ Financial records including net income, ratio of net income to total assets, working capital, fixed assets, operating environment existing inventory, accounts receivable and debts, audited financial statements for at least three years, credit report, loan agreements, capital budget, all debts and liabilities, inventory schedule, depreciation and amortization methods and accounting changes over five years, fixed and variable expense analysis, and analysis of gross margins.

- ☐ Real estate leases, deeds, mortgages, title policies, surveys, and zoning approvals, variances, or use permits.

- ☐ Insurance information including all coverage for facilities, workers' compensation, and claims over the last three years.

- ☐ Existing contracts with suppliers, customers, car and equipment rentals, work for hire, consulting, partners, subsidiaries, officers, directors, legal counsel, shareholders or affiliates, and financial agreements including loans, lines of credit, or promissory notes.

☐ Employee information including a list of positions, organizational charts, salaries, bonuses, résumés, health and welfare insurance plans, nondisclosure agreements, benefits, holiday, vacation and sick leave policies, personnel handbook, retirement plans, collective bargaining agreements, labor disputes, workers' compensation claims, stock option and purchase plans, and lawsuits for wrongful termination, discrimination, or harassment.

☐ Public relations, history, google searches, etc.

☐ Intellectual property including domestic and foreign patents and patent applications or clearance documents, trademarks and trade names, copyrights, inventions, and protected trade secrets.

☐ Environmental matters including audits of properties, hazardous substances used, disposal methods, permits and licenses, documents from the EPA as well as state and local regulatory agencies, litigation or investigations, and superfund exposure.

☐ Tax materials including U.S., state, local, and foreign tax returns, as well as state sales tax returns for at least three years, audit and revenue agency reports, tax settlement documents, employment tax filings, excise tax filings for three years, and any tax liens.

☐ Customer information including largest customers in terms of sales, unfilled orders, a report on any major customers who've been lost in recent years and why, and a list of major competitors.

Because legal and tax problems can be difficult to uncover until you dig into a business, it's always wise to add a "hold harmless and indemnify" clause to the purchase contract. The goal is to protect yourself from inheriting any major problems caused by the previous owner. It's also a good move to structure the deal so that you can retain the seller's insurance policies for a certain period. This gives you coverage until you can fully assess what your insurance needs will be. You will of course always need an experienced mergers and acquisitions (M&A) law firm.

PAVING YOUR OWN WAY

I will always be the first to tell you that Myrna deserves most of the credit for the success of our PeopleCare Heritage Centers. She had vital expertise (and PEP) thanks to her nursing degree and her many years of working in the field before we began buying them. She also proved to be an extremely good administrator. She oversaw all medical matters, human resources, and day-to-day operations. She was also raising our four kids, which may have been an even bigger job.

I only handled the financial matters, which gave me time to dive into an entirely new business just a few months after we bought our first residential care business in Texas. Or so I'd hoped!

A friend from Canada came down to visit us in 1979 and told me about his thriving business up there. He'd tapped into a big Ontario, Canada market for landscape and concrete pavers. Regular concrete driveways and sidewalks frequently tended to crack due to the extremes in temperature and the freeze-thaw cycle up north.

Concrete pavers or landscape paving stones are modular and tend to flex rather than crack and buckle in weather extremes. We discussed the fact that landscape pavers hadn't yet been introduced in Texas, even though concrete driveways and sidewalks there also tend to crack because of the big range in temperatures and the drought and seasonal rain cycles that cause the clay soil to shift.

We thought there was big growth potential for the manufacture and sales of landscaping pavers in Texas, so I invested $11,000 for a one-eighths share in the first round of capital raised in my friend's business. Myrna was successfully managing the nursing retirement centers, so I could devote time to this new business. Five or six years later, things started going so well, we went to Germany and purchased some very expensive and massive automated machinery. This saved labor costs and increased production as well.

We took out huge loans for each plant thinking we could handle the cost. Oops! Along came the recession of the late 1980s. Oil and real estate prices fell through the floor and our market collapsed.

During this challenging time, I found myself pumping more and more of my own money into the business. I was the only one putting more money in, so I decided to buy out my partner, allowing his family to move back to their business in Canada. For several years, I kept asking myself if I paid too much for his portion!

The company made it through the next five- or six-year downturn and when the economy turned around, Pavestone and I were poised for even greater growth. I will tell you, though, that there was a lot of sweat, tears, and fears as we struggled through this tough time.

My plan was to expand it into other areas of Texas and the Southwestern United States. Myrna was apprehensive about diving into another totally different and costly start-up so soon. She made the point that we already had our hands full managing and growing our nursing retirement centers.

She was also feeling torn because that business took so much of her time and pulled her away from our kids and their ever-growing list of activities. I convinced her that the potential market for concrete pavers was enormous in the United States. I also believed this was too good an opportunity to pass up, but it wasn't a small investment.

Over the next five years, I had to add more than $4 million to my original $11,000 investment. We already had purchased our second paving stone manufacturing press that compressed, vibrated, and compacted sand, aggregates, and cement to make the concrete pavers, and then we needed a new plant, with a lot of room to begin manufacturing. Our new automated plant was located on twenty-two acres in Grapevine, Texas. It became the headquarters of our company.

Over the next couple decades, we borrowed more than $200 million to build sixteen paver plants across the U.S. At our high point, our plants were producing over a billion paving stones a year for our customers, including Walmart and Home Depot.

After giving a plant tour to one of my young daughters one day, she pointed out that "Dad's factories just put sand, rock, and water in on one side, and money comes out on the other."

I only wish it were that simple. The challenge with this start-up was that it took time to reach $10 million in sales and become profitable, and we had much more capacity to quickly grow! Ideally, your start-up's revenues would grow more rapidly so that you begin generating significant cash flow.

I say that, but it is not easy. Pavestone took fourteen years to get to $10 million and five more years to get to $100 million. We grew by $100 million every three years after that until we reached $400 million.

My spreadsheet projections had us continuing to grow slightly below the 40 percent Compounded Annual Growth Rate (CAGR) we experienced annually in the '90s. However, a wise old M&A banker suggested, "Bob, oak trees don't grow to the sky, you know."

At the time I thought to myself, *That's the dumbest thing I've ever heard.* But he was right! We hit the wall thanks to the not so "Great Recession" that began in 2008.

The economy collapsed thanks to the subprime mortgage fiasco and all leveraged businesses were in trouble. Sales dropped dramatically. And the hits just kept on coming.

BIG AND SLOW VERSUS CLICK AND GO

Every start-up has its challenges. When you begin from scratch with a manufacturing business like Pavestone, there are huge upfront costs for machinery, equipment, and buildings, not to mention inventory, A/R, working capital, employees, and delivery vehicles for the heavy and cumbersome products.

This was a complex and expensive business to create, and while Pavestone eventually paid off in big ways, it was slow going for a long time. That's why I've been a bit envious, in a fatherly way, of some of the start-ups my kids have pulled off with considerably less money and complexity.

Our youngest daughter, for example, is a fashion, fitness, and lifestyle blogger, or "digital influencer," a career field that simply did not exist a few years ago, not to mention when I was her age. She was studying journalism, advertising, and fashion media at Southern Methodist University in Dallas when she began blogging in 2010.

She has always been interested in fashion, interior design, and a healthy lifestyle. To prepare as a blogger in that field, she also took classes at the Parson School of Design in New York City. She served internships with Chanel in Dallas, and the online fashion retailer Moda Operandi in New York.

Krystal became interested in blogging as a business thanks to two college friends, Amber Venz and Baxter Box, who were then dating but are now married. They told Krystal that if she featured products from major retail stores on her blog, the stores would pay her a commission on sales. I remember when Amber and Baxter came over to our house one afternoon and talked to me about the tech business they were starting from scratch. It seemed very foreign to me, but I encouraged them to go for it!

Their company, rewardStyle, which they started in 2011 in a studio apartment, builds technology that links shoppers, influencers, and retailers on social media. They work with thousands of brands and 150,000 influencers in more than 100 countries. They now have seven offices around the world, with a team of more than 350 employees. Krystal was one of the early influencers for what is now called LTK, valued at over $2 billion and drives over $3 billion in retail sales.

The start-up costs for blogging can be as low as a few thousand dollars. Basically, all you need is what nearly every young person already has—a decent computer, a digital camera, and a smartphone with a generous data plan and internet service. The only other additional items needed are not at all expensive: a custom URL from a provider like GoDaddy, or a free blogging service like Blogger.com or WordPress. Oh, yeah: You also need a work hard ethic, Krystal says!

You can spend substantially more if you hire a graphic designer to create a logo and make your webpage user friendly and dynamic. It's also true that most fashion bloggers don't have deals with major clothing retailers at first, so the cost for clothing and accessories can be substantial initially if you have to purchase them.

Our family blogging star tells me that some bloggers start out by renting clothing, buying it at secondhand stores, or buying, photographing, and then returning the items.

The more successful bloggers and influencers, like celebrities, athletes, and movie stars, have millions of followers. They can promote products and services by partnering up with designers and retailers who provide them with clothing and other goods.

KrystalSchlegel.com has around 100,000 followers, which is considered micro-influencer-status, she tells me. My daughter is constantly trying to raise her numbers, but the rules and regulations of this social media-based business are always changing as the websites, search engines, and retailers adjust their policies.

She has taken what began as a college website project and created a bonafide business with revenues in the six figures currently. Now married, she is focused on a healthy lifestyle, and that has attracted more collaborations. She has shown incredible discipline in building this cutting-edge business.

As I was putting this book together, Krystal and her husband, Luke Davis, a commercial real estate executive, collaborated on a beautiful and lively "project." Her name is Lake Grace Davis, and she was born on June 25, 2020.

A DEMANDING BUSINESS, NOT A HOBBY

Krystal loves this business because it matches her interests. She puts together outfits and models clothing and accessories she likes on her blog, mixing high-end pieces with more affordable selections. She provides links to the retailers and is paid commission on sales from partners including Nordstrom, Neiman Marcus, Lululemon, eBay, Walmart, and Bloomingdales, and more recently, Amazon. She also hosts store openings and other fashion, fitness, and lifestyle events and blogs about them for her readers.

As Krystal is quick to point out, however, "This is not a hobby. It's a twenty-four-seven, no-days-off job because you need to be working during the hours when others are shopping, including weekends and holidays."

The income you can earn depends on many factors, including how long you've been blogging, how many followers you have, and how much fresh content you provide that can be shared.

Like most businesses, the more work you are willing to put into it, the more success you will likely have. "You must have a good work ethic and manage your time wisely, and you have to stay on top of changing fashions and technology," my daughter says. "I think I work more hours than many of my friends with careers in other fields."

Krystal wants to keep growing her business, but she notes that the rules and regulations are constantly changing, so there is always a bit of uncertainty in the blogging business, just as there is in nearly any other. There are no guarantees in business. There are always risks, and successful entrepreneurs accept that fact, while doing their best to minimalize those risks.

"The biggest thing I've learned is to be a helpful resource for other women, and they can talk to me as a friend, recommending things and helping with healthy habits. My husband has been pictured on the blog occasionally as well. Whenever we get paid for a joint campaign sponsored post, we use it for a travel fund to do fun trips."

ENTREPRENEURIAL GENES

Krystal is the youngest in a line of Schlegel family entrepreneurs. All of our children have enjoyed entrepreneurial careers while raising their families, and I think because they grew up watching their mother and me create and grow our own businesses.

Our daughter Kari has a very determined approach to business, much like her mother. She is not afraid to be straightforward. She is a hard worker and determined to succeed. She has never met a challenge she can't handle.

Kari earned her undergraduate degree from Southern Methodist University with the goal of becoming an elementary school teacher. That surprised us, but after doing her student teaching stint, she decided maybe teaching was not the best fit for her.

She considered law school, thinking that might be her niche. She decided not to follow that path after learning from her friends, who were lawyers, that it wasn't the sort of lifestyle she would enjoy. Instead, she decided to pursue an MBA from SMU, and she moved forward to a very lucrative career in residential real estate. In this profession, she can basically set her own hours and still raise a family.

My daughter and her team partners quickly became sales leaders with a top real estate firm in Dallas. Of course, she has the genes of two entrepreneurial parents, so Kari didn't stop there.

She soon launched her own online clothing business for children called "JoJo Mommy." "After trying without success to find high-quality, classic children's clothing in the U.S., she decided to launch an online clothing business with high-quality European brands. It was such a successful venture that she later opened a small retail shop within a friend's business for those who preferred to visit a brick-and-mortar store.

Our children have a gift for finding opportunities to develop businesses, and like their parents, they often have several businesses operating at the same time. You have to be skilled at time management to do that because all businesses require a great deal of attention and energy if they are to succeed.

Currently, Kari operates her own real estate investing firm, an upscale retail outlet for JoJo Mommy's walk-in customers, and a small warehouse fulfillment center for her growing web business, jojomommy.com.

Kari believes that having diverse business enterprises works well for her, in part, because they seem to open up other entrepreneurial opportunities on a regular basis. She and her husband Troy do not lack for things to talk about at the dinner table with all of their businesses and shared interests!

BIG SISTER AND BIG ROLE MODEL

Like her sisters, our daughter Kim has built a multifaceted career around her interests and experiences, which I heartily recommend—especially for young entrepreneurs with a passion for one field or another.

Kim has created an entrepreneurial empire with retail businesses, media channels, and nine published books. Her first start-up was inspired by her participation in the Idlewild Debutante Ball, a major social event in Dallas. While planning the celebrations, Kim and Myrna discovered that there were very few sources in the area that rented high-quality crystal, china, and linens for her party.

Kim has refined tastes. She graduated from Southern Methodist University in art history, and she was continuing her art studies in the Christie's Connoisseurship Program in New York City. Since the Dallas area party rentals were so expensive and not the quality she wanted, my angel bought the party items wholesale, much to my chagrin. But it turned out to be a good move.

When she moved back to Dallas, her friends kept asking to borrow those high-end party supplies for their own events. So Kim decided to turn it into a rental business charging market rates. This led to the launch of RSVP Soiree Luxury Events Rentals.

The venture had high startup costs because so must inventory was required, which was a little painful for her financial backer—me. But it helped Kim establish a brand as a lifestyle entrepreneur before she sold it in 2006. The business is still operating successfully under its current owners, one of whom started under Kim's ownership as the person responsible for answering phones.

Kim moved on to new opportunities, including a book deal. She was way ahead of her dad in becoming an author. Kim was just twenty-four years old when she wrote *The Pleasure of Your Company: Entertaining in High Style*. The success of that book led to several party books, one about pooches and another that sprang out of her wedding, *The Wedding Workbook: A Time Saving Guide for a Busy Bride.* Her ninth book comes out in spring 2022.

Her books brought invitations for book signings all over the country, which led to the creation of her own segments as an entertainment expert on the NBC's *Today* show. So far, she's written another eight books on lifestyle and party planning topics.

Kim also hosted her own live television show in Dallas for more than a year but found that it consumed too much of her time. For ten years, she served as the editor-at-large of *Southern Living* magazine.

In 2015, her entrepreneurial spirit kicked in again when she and her college sorority sister, who had a calligraphy business, created a line of table linens that brings classic designs to the modern hostess.

Their line, Halo Home by KSW, created linens and popular emoji cocktail napkins sold in more than 200 stores across the country. In 2018, the pair sold that business to Mariana Barran de Goodall, the founder of Hibiscus Linens.

By the way, Kim calls herself a "serial start-up and sell-off entrepreneur" because she has launched and sold so many of her ventures. She has even sold and later re-purchased one business. Like everyone in our family, she loves the entrepreneurial game.

Kim's books and retail experience have established her reputation as an expert in all things related to lifestyle, from entertaining to fashion. Her strong sense of style led to an opportunity to create a collection of dresses, shoes, and children's clothing in collaboration with Antonio Melani for Dillard's department stores.

I marvel her entrepreneurial drive and her ability to balance work and family with such grace. All of my daughters have inherited those skills, and their beauty, from their mother. Today, Kim serves in a high-profile role as the Fashion and Lifestyle Ambassador for NorthPark Center, a shopping destination in Dallas

Along with her busy career, she is the mother of two of my wonderful grandchildren. She has a wide following on Instagram, and her websites Kimberlywhitman.com and ShopKSW.com.

I share these stories of our entrepreneurial family as a proud father, and also as inspiration to aspiring entrepreneurs as well as entrepreneurs who face challenges in their businesses. We've had our share, certainly. The secret is to never give up on your dreams. Success will come to those who persevere in pursuing their entrepreneurial dreams.

THE SPIN-OFF

Earlier, I mentioned that a third way to start your own business is to spin one off from an existing business, whether it's a division within a company where you work, or a concept for a company that serves as a supplier or customer to your employer.

At Pavestone, we started a separate logistics division in the late 1990s to lower our costs for shipping heavy and often cumbersome landscape and building products to our 10,000+ customer locations nationwide, including Home Depot and Walmart. Each spring and summer, our fleet of trucks delivered products to those big-box retail stores almost every day, as well as to homes and other construction sites. The freight part of our operation had grown to be a $20 million business within Pavestone.

It began with our first bobtail delivery truck in 1980 and evolved into an in-house distribution system with hundreds of our own eighteen-wheel tractor trailer rigs. They serviced our customers, delivering from Pavestone's manufacturing plants across the country. In 2003, we incorporated Bedrock Logistics, LLC into our own logistics division to synthesize our freight transportation system, including our own fleet, contract carriers, and third-party logistics providers.

The mission was to reduce the number of empty trailer trips made after dropping off a load (known in the trade as "empty back haul miles"), which accounted for half of total trucking costs for Pavestone and most factory truck fleets industrywide. We also worked to improve delivery times and minimize overall outbound and inbound transportation costs.

KEEP ON TRUCKING

When we sold the rest of Pavestone to Quikrete, I used Bedrock as the platform for my next venture. Entrepreneurs are typically big fans of this method for launching new businesses because it is usually less expensive and lower risk than either starting a business from scratch or buying and growing an existing company.

This spin-off was easier than many because I was selling the primary business and keeping a division of it. In other cases, a business owner may feel that some part of his operation has evolved in ways that no longer make it an essential part of the existing company, yet it still has the potential to develop into a profitable business on its own.

There are many options with this form of start-up. Many entrepreneurs can't help themselves from spinning off a new business even as they continue to operate their main business or several businesses. When they see an opportunity, they are inclined to jump on it.

Yet, most successful entrepreneurs still will take the time to do a thorough evaluation of the risks involved by checking out potential competitors, researching market trends, assessing the economic environment, and putting together a business plan that lays out the costs, as well as staffing and equipment needs, required technologies, equipment, office, and manufacturing space.

You always should ask yourself if engineering a spin-off makes sense strategically for your overall business interests. You wouldn't want to chop off a highly profitable division or essential operation and risk crippling your existing company.

Make sure you have the resources to grow the spin-off without draining cash from the more valuable enterprise. And again, don't spin off a new business that you might grow bored with after a year or two; make sure it's something you care about and will enjoy for years to come.

Most spin-offs have existing products and infrastructure, a proven market with an existing customer base, and assets that make it easier to find investors or secure bank loans. It is also true that once you start spinning off a business, there always seems to be more spinning required. This has proven the case with Bedrock Logistics.

We began as a stand-alone, debt-free, third-party logistics provider.

Originally, I saw this as a company that would continue to transport pavestones and similar materials because that was our area of expertise. As we got into the market, however, we learned that new technologies were available that opened up opportunities for our company to serve as a matchmaker between truckers looking for loads and businesses searching for trucks to transport all types of goods.

ON THE ROAD, JUST NEED A LOAD

My elevator pitch description of Bedrock is that we want to be the Uber for the transportation industry, matching trucks and drivers with those seeking a ride for their products. This match game is more challenging because there aren't enough trucks available for all of the goods that need to be moved on any given day—and companies only want to use truck owners who are insured and reliable.

We work with companies to minimize the empty return trips their trucks often make. For so many businesses, after a full truckload is delivered, there is an opportunity to be more efficient and load up with goods that need to go the direction they are travelling anyways.

Bedrock Logistics can make them more efficient by finding loads for them to bring back. We earn a commission for making that connection, with the promise that we will find a trucker who will do it for less because he doesn't want to run empty. We've invested in sophisticated transportation management systems software and built an experienced operations team. Bedrock now selects from tens of thousands of qualified carriers that we have accounts with who are "on the road in need of a load."

We offer what we think is the most reliable and efficient freight logistics service to manufacturers and distributors throughout the United States, Canada, and Mexico. In our first year as an independent company, Bedrock had revenues of $13 million.

Our corporate headquarters is in Dallas and we currently have additional service locations in Orlando and Houston, providing coverage from East to West coasts, including Canada and Mexico. Bedrock currently has nearly 100 employees. We track every truck across the country on computer screens. We also have three IT guys who focus on upgrading the software at every opportunity, so we stay on the cutting edge.

Bedrock is all software and computers, which I find fascinating, because when I was in school there were no small business computers. We were still using hand calculators in some of my classes. I had about ten years of manual accounting experience in high school and college. Accountants didn't have desktop computers until after I'd sold my accounting firm in 1980, and in the 1970s, the first models were as big as a house and cost millions.

My first personal business computer was a TRS-80 from Radio Shack. It had a whopping four kilobytes of memory and a floppy disk drive. I had to lug it around between home and the office while also carrying all of those floppy disks. Today I love being surrounded by all of the serious IT geeks at Bedrock, and it is a great deal of fun to be involved with this Pavestone spin-off, which has turned into a major enterprise.

I am having the time of my life, to tell you the truth. Friends and family tease me that in Bedrock, I may have finally found the perfect match for my math-maniac brain because it's like playing with a giant sudoku puzzle every day and I get to work with a lot of spreadsheets.

Being excited and engaged is important to me. It's the reason I haven't retired. Business keeps my blood flowing. Will I slow down? Never, I hope! I find it hard to give up the entrepreneurial life. I just truly enjoy building businesses, creating jobs and opportunities, and being part of a dynamic company that supports lots of families.

Okay, I admit it: Sometimes I may take my entrepreneurial love a little too far. After I sold my paving stone business, I told Myrna that I had to start another one or I'd die. She thought that was a bit dramatic, but I like to keep busy.

I don't have many time-consuming weekend hobbies. I am not a golfer or a hunter so, even though I'm in what many consider to be my retirement years, I still want to keep working. So you can call me "Bedrock Bob," because I plan to keep on trucking until I get a call to join my angels upstairs. This passion is what you need to have for success. Before you launch your own business, remember you need to ask yourself if you are okay working on Saturday instead of being on the golf course.

Chapter Four

FINANCING YOUR DREAM BUSINESS

Back in my most successful days with Pavestone, a brilliant guy who worked for one of our suppliers came to me with a proposition to start his own company. Pavestone had been his biggest customer and we had a very good relationship. He is an engineer, and I considered him a rock star in our industry.

We previously had discussed the need for the service his new company would provide. I had encouraged him, so when he came to me, I agreed to guarantee his bank note to raise start-up capital. He didn't have to put up any money. I guaranteed a $1 million bank loan! In return, I became owner of a portion of his company and receive a nice discount on his products for Pavestone.

I still sit on his board and go to meetings annually. I also receive nice dividends from his business, which he has worked hard to build and improve over the years. Our business relationship has been mutually beneficial and both of us are very pleased with how it has worked out. This one has developed well for over twenty years now as we reduced our raw material costs and still make a tidy return on our original, risky loan guarantee. That doesn't always happen in these situations, which makes it all the more rewarding and a nice win-win for everyone!

I have been on both sides of these "angel" financing deals. In my early days as an entrepreneur, I had to borrow money. Now, I'm often the source of funding for people and projects that I believe in. I tend to trust people until they prove themselves unworthy of trust. I prefer to see fellow entrepreneurs in the best light possible, and sometimes I've been wrong, but more often, I've been right.

Borrowing and investing money is always a risky venture, but it is often essential for starting and growing a business. Few aspiring entrepreneurs have all of the available funds necessary to launch their first business and keep them going through the start-up and early-growth phases. Finding the money to start a first business is almost always the biggest hurdle we face. The next hurdle is then maintaining a consistent cash flow to grow your business in its early years.

A key thing to consider before you start your initial phase of fundraising for a business is that the amount of money raised by entrepreneurs early on is often inversely correlated to their long-term success. This means that those who raise less tend to thrive more with a much higher Internal Rate of Return (IRR), which is the annual rate of growth an investment generates.

Why is that? Well, it's usually because these entrepreneurs tend to be more thoughtful and resourceful when it comes to initial investing to prove their concept will work. They also build and maintain cash flow and profits without taking on any debt or partners. You learn quickly that "cash flow" is the most important part of running any business!

The stereotypical depiction of entrepreneurs is that they are risk-takers who are comfortable taking on substantial debt. There is certainly truth in that portrayal. After I've proven my concept worked and I have a successful business model, I've taken on tens of millions in personal debt to build businesses worth hundreds of millions.

I will admit, however, that I've made mistakes in taking on too much debt, bringing in partners, and personally guaranteeing loans. I want to spare you the pain that results from making the same mistake when financing your business or businesses.

Any time you take out a loan, no matter where it comes from, you set yourself up for sleepless nights. I know this all too well. Early on in my entrepreneurial career, I had to borrow $500,000 from a bank and my father co-signed with me. This was our down payment on our first nursing retirement centers in Texas. A loss would have represented a huge part of our net worth!

Myrna and I were still in our twenties with young children, and we were buying a facility that was modern but only half-full, very poorly managed, and a thousand miles away. We'd already sold our home in Canada to finance our first nursing retirement centers there. So, we rented a house in Canada and an apartment in Dallas as we tested out the U.S. market.

Borrowing with personal guarantees meant risk was piled upon risk. If our entry into the Texas market had not succeeded, it would not have been pretty.

My parents weren't at all thrilled that we'd decided to shift our business from Canada to the United States. They feared we might move there someday. So, things were tense enough when we sat down for the closing with the bankers and the title company in a big downtown Dallas bank in an office high-rise on July 31, 1979. The tension worsened considerably after we signed all the paperwork and our lawyer said: "Where's your money?"

I had arranged a $500,000 bank loan, and we had all personally guaranteed it. The bank was supposed to have wired it earlier that day.

Or at least that's what Myrna and I believed.

"It was sent to you," we said.

The banker gave us a look that seemed to ask, "Are these Canadian kids scamming me?"

Panic set in. My father had trusted us despite his reservations about this foreign deal. How could we tell him the money had been lost?

"Maybe the wire hasn't come through yet?" Myrna said hopefully.

The bank officer left the room to make a call.

He returned and said, "There is no wire. I told our people to keep looking."

We walked out and called our banker in Canada from a pay phone. Our legs were shaking. Who were these Dallas bankers? Had we been taken in?

"I sent it by wire hours ago," he said.

We returned to suspicious stares from the bankers in the closing room.

"Let's just give it a while. These international wire transfers can take longer than most," said one of the lawyers.

One hour passed.

Then two.

We paced the room, biting our nails while trying to show confidence.

Another long hour passed, and finally, a call came in to our banker: "We found it! It's here!"

I wish I could say that we felt great relief. Instead, my wife and I wondered even more if we were making a huge mistake and putting too much at risk by borrowing such a large amount from the bank. We celebrated by sleeping on the floor of our new, unfurnished Dallas apartment that night, as we didn't want to commit to renting furniture until we were positive our deal was closed.

Now, as things turned out, we were able to turn around those first nursing retirement centers in Dallas very quickly. In fact, we refinanced in Texas and paid back our Canadian bank in full after eighteen months. We even managed to pay my dad a little extra for his faith in us. We were all grateful, but it was accomplished through lots of hard work, travel, and blood, sweat and tears (oh yeah, and PEP!)

FINDING THE MONEY

The entrepreneur's two traditional choices for finding outside funding to start a business are to secure either an equity raise that involves selling a piece of the business in exchange for start-up cash, or to take on debt with a straight-up loan of some kind.

A third source is from existing customers of your company's products. Customers are always looking for better deals and would love to have guaranteed supply agreements. Perhaps they could invest in your company or help guarantee debt like I did for our Pavestone supplier!

The first method often requires giving up some portion of the control of your business, or at least it invites meddling (otherwise known as "needed third-party advice," depending on your perspective). The second can involve sleepless nights even in the best cases. In the worst cases, it can lead to financial disaster.

Before I decide on taking any source of funding for my businesses, I always do a detailed and realistic survey of the three possible scenarios that could occur:

1. The best case

2. The probable case

3. The worst case

Just keep that in mind and put it on paper whenever you are looking at outside financing for your business. I will provide you with examples of all three in this book. Your traditional choices for financing a business include:

- Self-financing through savings, tapping your 401k, home equity, or second mortgage

- You have probably read about entrepreneurs who maxed out their credit cards to finance a start-up, but I would never advise doing that. It's just too costly given the rates they charge.

- Borrowing from friends and family

- Loans from banks, online lenders (a.k.a. "cloud-funding"), or credit unions

- Venture capital loans

- Private equity loans

- Loans or micro-loans from government groups like the Small Business Administration or small business investment corporations

- Public options

Certainly, after you've proven your concept and convinced the market of your growth potential and scalability, you can do like Steve Jobs, Bill Gates, Michael Dell, Jeff Bezos, Elon Musk, and many other billionaires have done on Wall Street!

There are pros and cons—and risks—involved with any form of borrowing, especially if it involves taking on heavy debt or bringing in outside investors who likely have their own agendas. Before you go to any outside source for funding, I highly recommend that you work up a realistic assessment of what your start-up costs will be. There are many of these start-up cost worksheet templates available online, including on the website of the U.S. Small Business Administration.

If you are leaving your day job to start the new business from scratch, remember to figure in your living expenses for the start-up period. The power bill and all of your other living costs will still have to be paid.

This is fun for me because I love crunching numbers, and if there is any time to "be like Bob," it's at this point in your entrepreneurial launch. Do your best to be accurate and include all potential costs. You won't be doing yourself any favors if you present your estimates to potential investors or loan officers and they laugh at you or rip it up because you've been unrealistic or overly optimistic.

SELF-FUNDING YOUR START-UP

In a perfect world, all entrepreneurs could tap their own savings to finance every start-up business. Self-financing is appealing because you avoid taking on debt at an early stage and you retain control over your business without the burden of meddling investors or partners. Business owners with skin in the game also find it is easier to attract bank loans and investors later on.

The problem with this is if you don't have the funds, you can't do the self-funding, but don't give up! Personal guarantees will probably be necessary on most bank loans, but if you don't have huge resources, the risks are not as high. Some entrepreneurs tend to believe they have nothing to lose. That may not be wise.

When I was a rookie CPA, a client in the construction business told me that he never worried about personal guarantees because he had so few assets. "What are they going to do, take my dishes?" he said.

That is not a healthy mindset, either, and it is a bad habit to get into, because if it all goes well one day, you *will* have a lot to lose. It is true that for those just starting out with their own ventures, finding the initial capital is a challenge, and personal guarantees will be necessary!

Most start-ups need a substantial sum to get rolling, whether you build a business from the ground up or buy an existing company.

BORROWING FROM FRIENDS AND FAMILY

As my story about briefly losing our $500,000 guaranteed loan illustrates, borrowing from friends and family can be a nerve-wracking experience, too. Let's face it: If you borrow money from a bank and things go sour, you don't have to worry about sitting across from your loan officer at Thanksgiving, Christmas, and every other family event for years to come.

So, my advice is, first of all, to make sure the family member or friend loaning you the money understands all the risks involved. Also make sure that they aren't loaning you so much money that they could go down with you if your star-tup never gets off the ground. This is not the time to bet the farm.

You may desperately want to have a business of your own, but don't pressure friends or family members into helping you achieve that dream. No guilt trips! No reminding them of all the joy you've brought into their lives. Do not prey on their emotions. This should be a professional business deal with all the proper legal agreements drawn up, signed, and sealed.

Myrna and I still have nightmares and flashbacks over all that could have gone wrong when my dad cosigned. I never did it again, needless to say. Now, I have *loaned* sizeable sums to my own children and others, but the amount was never so large that it would have endangered our futures if their ventures failed.

There are precautions you can take to lessen the risk and offer at least some protection for your friends, your family members, and yourself when borrowing money from those close to you. I recommend you have a lawyer draft a promissory note, the agreement securing the amount of the loan, and the repayment terms. The note should provide not only the amount and the terms of payment but also the date it comes due, the interest rate, and a regular payment schedule.

Once you and your lender agree on all of the above, the work is just beginning. Remember also to have a Plan B in place in case your venture fails and you can't come up with the money for repayment as scheduled.

I have borrowed from family and friends, and I have loaned money to family and friends, as well as invested in their businesses. Still, I advise being cautious when entering into financial deals with those closest to you. You always should ask yourself if you really want to put a friendship or relationship in jeopardy, because sometimes you have to make tough decisions and that could be difficult when you have personal ties to your investors.

For example, Pavestone started out small, with an $11,000 investment, but we ultimately had to borrow millions to build it. Eventually our partners weren't contributing as much and we bought them out.

BORROWING FROM TRADITIONAL LENDERS

Banks, credit unions, and commercial and online lenders provide a valuable service and can be great resources for entrepreneurs as long as we always keep in mind that they are in business to make money, too, just like us. And they make money when we borrow money and pay it back on their schedule at an interest rate they set.

In other words, they aren't our friends even though they may seem friendly enough. It's all business with them, which is understandable, though sometimes we mistakenly think they are close friends. There is truth in the saying that bankers are always there with an umbrella for you when it is sunny outside, but not when it is raining.

If you take nothing else away from this book, please always follow this rule: If a bank won't give you a line of credit without demanding a personal guarantee, then don't do it unless you have nothing to lose or you are prepared to actually lose other valuable assets.

I've done it, and I've regretted it deeply. I will write more about this mistake later, but basically, we needed money to build more concrete plants to keep growing Pavestone, which was then a thriving business.

The banks were willing to give me that money, but only if I personally guaranteed one specific, smaller piece of the loans. This was in a boom period when such transactions were very common. No one thought much of personally guaranteeing business loans back then.

But boom times don't last forever, and the boom came down on me when the economy turned ugly in 2008 and the banks demanded their money back. People now call it the Great Recession. I could have declared bankruptcy, but I believe in taking responsibility for my debts. In retrospect, if I had borrowed that money without a personal guarantee, it would have been much easier to negotiate repayment terms over time.

Lesson learned, and I hope my mistake will prevent you from ever taking out a loan with a personal guarantee, because if you default even for reasons beyond your control, you and your family will suffer.

Now, keep in mind that this advice is coming from an entrepreneur who has borrowed hundreds of millions of dollars from bankers. I did it to build a business worth hundreds of millions more—until it wasn't.

If you are just starting out as an entrepreneur and don't have a proven track record, every bank will require some form of collateral to guarantee repayment. Just always know what you are risking.

Angel investors

This book is about how my life has been blessed by guardian angels who have come to my rescue many times throughout my life. Those angels, some heavenly, some human, have helped me in those times when my health and physical well-being was somehow endangered. I caution you, though: Do not confuse angel investors with guardian angels.

Angel investors are a different breed. You look to them when the financial health of your business needs a boost. They are not heaven sent. They are human, and they can be good or bad angels, so you have to be very careful when you accept financial assistance from them.

In exchange for investing in your business, they will of course want a percentage. Don't make the mistake of giving away too much of your company, though, because you can lose effective control of it quickly. And you may need to come back for more funds down the road, so you need to keep some for future bargaining power.

The popular television show *Shark Tank*, or the Canadian version, *Dragon's Den*, offers an introduction to the world of angel investors, but keep in mind it's more show business than real business. By watching these shows, you can learn a thing or two about how to make an "elevator pitch" to potential investors with a brief explanation of your business and your goals for it.

When pitching your company or business concept, you really need to give an honest picture of its current state and potential to succeed. If you aren't good at crunching numbers and speaking the language of business financials, you might be wise to have your accountant handle that part of the pitch.

The "shark" analogy can be quite accurate in the real world if things don't go as planned, which is often. Sometimes the investors may decide they can run the business better than you can and try to take control away from you or sell the company out from under you.

When my Pavestone company hit hard times after the Federal Trade Commission (FTC) and the Hart-Scott-Rodino Act blocked our sale at the start of the Great Recession (which I will elaborate on later), we accepted an investment from another entrepreneurial family who convinced us that they wanted a long-term partnership that would benefit both their children and grandchildren and ours for generations.

It went well for the first year and a half of the investment. It seemed like angels had arrived when they became a 50 percent partner. However, as the Recession ended up being greater and longer than anyone had anticipated and as it continued to pound our sales, especially in the big-box retailers, things got darker.

At one point, this angel investor lost its wings when they proposed to buy us out for a small fraction of our share of the original $540 million we had contracted to sell it for three years earlier. It is pretty tough when you have built a business over thirty years and someone else steps in and tries to take it over.

Because of the relationships I had developed with my company's managers and employees, not one of them left me during the tough times. For most of them, it would have been easier to take positions with other companies when the future of our company was unknown. The fact that they stayed with me is something I will always appreciate. That was a very tough time for me. We had to do some downsizing, and I am always more interested in growing than shrinking a business.

The challenge increased when my perceived angel investors dropped a bomb on me when they sold their entire family company, including their share of Pavestone. I only found out because my assistant saw a Google alert that morning saying that Pavestone had been sold in part of a larger deal. It was devasting. Especially from a partner who had talked about, promised, and demanded 100 percent transparency!

Myrna said I was like a zombie after that news hit. My staff rallied and they were fantastic.

Keep in mind that angel investors don't come to your aid for altruistic reasons. They hope to make money, as they should, by investing into your company and getting a higher return than they'd get elsewhere, usually expecting double-digit percent returns.

That's not to say that they can't give your business a needed boost. Often, they also will have expertise in your field that can be beneficial. Just make sure you are careful and learn all you can about this person's reputation and practices.

Angel investors can be a blessing and they can be a curse. I have dealt with both types, and I've also been on both sides, because I've been an angel investor myself. I think of angel investors as individuals who are willing to put their own funds into entrepreneurial businesses while serving as advisors and mentors.

Unlike professional venture capital or private equity (PE) groups, which may have a pool of money in the hundreds of millions and even billions of dollars of OPM (Other People's Money), individual angel investors generally aren't working with such huge sums to invest.

Venture capital partnerships and banking firms are less likely to invest in start-ups. They look for businesses with growth potential and a proven track record that can give them a return of 30 percent or more.

While angel investors are often successful professionals, such as entrepreneurs, doctors, lawyers, accountants, and retired corporate leaders, they don't have to be billionaires or multimillionaires. They can simply be people with savings who are looking for a good return on their investment capital.

WHAT ANGEL INVESTORS WANT TO SEE
IN YOUR BUSINESS

I enjoy helping entrepreneurs build their dream businesses and create security for their families because I know what it is like to struggle and to succeed. I look for dynamic entrepreneurs who are fully engaged, honest, and excited about their ventures. I am willing to mentor them if they are open to my guidance, but I don't hover over them.

I expect them to know the financials and the market inside and out. They should also have a well-developed business plan along with a good management team who shares their vision and develops a step-by-step plan for growing their companies and for exiting them, too.

Like most people, I want to make money on my investments. So, I look for businesses that have the potential for amazing growth, so that after five to seven years, I can earn a nice multiple of the investment.

You probably won't be surprised to learn that one of my favorite places to find worthy investments is at the school that we have endowed to encourage and develop entrepreneurs, the Schlegel Centre for Entrepreneurship and Social Innovation at Wilfrid Laurier University in my hometown of Waterloo, Canada.

One of the more recent start-up projects caught my interest: Guard-Ex, a company that makes driver impairment screening devices for public safety and law enforcement. It was founded by students in the center's LaunchPad incubator, along with a graduate student and another student from outside the program. They launched the company in 2018, targeting the market for an accurate and unbiased roadside impairment screening device for law enforcement.

Their timing for this market is especially fortuitous because the legalization of cannabis across Canada and many states will likely increase law enforcement's need for this more sophisticated device. The founders have since presented their prototype to the Ontario Association of Chiefs of Police. As of this writing, they are creating a pilot program to test the Guard-Ex on the road.

I invested in this start-up because I was impressed by their innovative approach. They developed their universal impairment screening device with the help of machine learning to screen for real-time impairment. Their device automates the manual process conducted by law enforcement officers using the traditional methods. Guard-Ex also uses physiological indicators that measure eye movement and body temperature instead of the standard method of measuring chemicals from saliva or breath.

Now, many entrepreneurs have pitched me over the years to invest in their companies and I've invested a lot of money, but these innovators are filling a market need that is critical to the public's safety and welfare. They are smart and driven and I know they'll do well, especially with all of the coaching and mentoring they will receive from the LaunchPad incubator team. I may offer guidance now and then, too, since I've put in $500,000 for 25 percent and will probably put in more as an angel investor.

I believe this could be a huge, multimillion-dollar business if this product works as intended. The growing cannabis market will create a great demand for it. I also see this as a positive social impact investment that will improve public safety for everyone. I will offer more on this philosophy of investing for the greater good in a later chapter.

Chapter Five

BUILDING A TEAM

Just as I was preparing to write this chapter on the challenges of recruiting, hiring, and managing a team for your business, I received a letter from one of my great hires. His note reminded me that one of the most rewarding aspects of being an entrepreneur is creating jobs and having a positive impact on the lives of the men and women who work for you.

The letter was from Carlos, one of my hires in the early 2000s at Pavestone. He is a native of Colombia who developed a love of the United States first as a tourist, then as a student, and, eventually, as a resident.

Carlos and his wife Lina first lived in the U.S. together while studying for their MBAs in 2000. Carlos had already earned geological and civil engineering degrees in his native country. He had also worked in Colombia as a quality engineer and plant manager for Argos, the cement mix manufacturer, for nearly seven years.

We had a lot of engineers at Pavestone running our high-tech plants, designing new products, doing quality control, studying the chemical reaction of different cementitious materials and mix designs, and implementing lean management techniques.

At that point, Carlos was already active in trade organizations and kept up on industry developments, so, as he puts it, "I was already a committed cement head."

He had nearly completed his MBA degree in Louisiana when Carlos began sending out résumés and applications, hoping to land a job in the U.S. He applied for a plant manager position in Pavestone's Houston plant, and as soon as I saw all of his experience in our industry and the level of education he'd attained, I grabbed the phone.

Carlos remembers the moment. He was in his graduate student office in Louisiana when his phone rang, and I immediately launched into my pitch.

"It was Bob himself, which shocked me. He started to interview me right away, and my first impression was not only how fast he talks, but how quickly he decided to have his team talk to me," Carlos recalls.

I had Carlos interview with the general manager of our Louisiana plant, which wasn't far from his campus. He made such a good impression that I immediately set up interviews with our operational managers and senior vice presidents in Dallas, as well as the general manager of the Houston plant.

"Things happened at light speed," Carlos says.

We decided to hire him for our Dallas plant. This was in 2003. He was thirty years old and he notes, "I'd been married to Lina for two years when I married Pavestone and we started a family together."

Carlos moved up quickly at Pavestone. He weathered both the economic boom and then the recession with us, and then he stayed with the company after I sold it. As of 2022, he remains with the company in their Atlanta headquarters, where he is corporate quality manager for the Pavestone division that makes concrete pavers.

I hadn't heard from him in years when his note arrived as I was writing this chapter. Needless to say, it was great to hear from him, and to get the news that one of his greatest dreams had been fulfilled:

Dear Mr. Schlegel,

It is with great joy and a profound sense of gratitude that I can inform you that as of yesterday Lina and I became U.S. Citizens! We will always remember you and be grateful for your key support in our immigration process. I'm also thankful for the opportunity of being part of the great team that you put together and being inspired by great leaders like you.

Ultimately Bob, you had a very significant positive impact on our lives and the history of our family. Please say hello to Myrna and extend our heartfelt gratitude to her. May God keep blessing you and your family.

Thank you again Bob,

Sincerely,
Carlos, Lina, Matias, and Lucas

It was heartwarming to hear from Carlos, and his note was interesting on a couple of levels. On one level, I could relate to his excitement about getting his U.S. citizenship because just a few months earlier, I achieved the same goal after working with a green card for nearly thirty-five years!

I also was grateful to have helped Carlos begin what has been a very successful career and life in his adopted country. His story is just a terrific example of why entrepreneurship is such an important aspect of our global economy, because our successful businesses contribute jobs as well as income, and those jobs, in return, help employees and their families thrive—often for generations to come.

By the way, you should never let a top 10 percenter like Carlos get away. Top talent is hard to find, and those with highly specialized skills are vital to any business.

After congratulating Carlos and catching up with him and his family, I asked him if he had any thoughts on what I should share in this chapter on building a team. This is his response:

Bob, you helped me so much with my career and you were so support-ive of my efforts to become a citizen, and I think every entrepreneur can learn so much from you about team-building. You used to send us business and management books and articles to encourage us to keep growing and learning throughout our careers. You encour-aged us to never become stagnant, to read and to work on cogni-tive improvement and gathering all the tools we needed because you believed the learning process never ends no matter how long you've been doing a job, or whatever job you are doing.

I still use many of the things I learned from the material you shared. I also think you are very good at hiring the right people for the right jobs. That sounds simple enough, but we all know of brilliant and professional people who become frustrated and ineffective because they are in the wrong position at the wrong time. It can be a com-plete disaster when that happens. You put a lot of effort into always making sure you had the right person in the right position and the right location. If someone was struggling, you always tried to find a better fit to make the most of the individual's talents and knowledge.

Another thing: You hear a lot about the importance of corporate values these days, and I'm always struck by the fact that when I worked for you, it was a given that everything would be handled according to the highest values and highest standards. It was just never questioned. The example you set made us want to live by the same values. It set the bar high, not only for managers, but also for all employees.

We also always knew that you valued your employees and wanted the best for them. For example, you enforced a strict tobacco-free pol-icy in the company and supported those who wanted to stop using nicotine. In the process, you probably saved a lot of lives, not to men-tion a lot of money, for people who quit. That spoke volumes to us.

BUILDING THE BEST POSSIBLE TEAM

As Carlos noted, I strongly believe in finding the right person for the right job at the right time. Sometimes, that means I've had to move the job to wherever that person wants to live. Someone asked me recently why my Bedrock Logistics company, based in Dallas, has satellite offices in Orlando and in Houston. In both cases, we opened offices there to accommodate very good employees.

The Houston office was opened by one of our managing directors who had been working for us many years in Dallas. When he and his wife became grandparents, they wanted to be closer to their grandchildren in Houston. He came into my office one day to offer his resignation, but when he told me why, I suggested he just open a satellite office in Houston and continue to work for us. I thought highly of him, and as someone who always talks about the value of family ties, I could hardly blame him for wanting to see his grand-kids more often.

I believe entrepreneurs have to be flexible when it comes to hiring great people. I do anything I can to keep them, as long as they are enthusiastic and productive in their jobs. You can't grow a business into a highly profitable enterprise without a whole lot of help from a team with a wide range of skills and expertise.

WHEN TO MAKE NEW HIRES

That said, I try not to hire more people than we need at any given time, even during periods of rapid growth for my companies. I'd rather wait a little bit too long than bring more employees on board too soon and have to deal with all of the additional expense of adding to the payroll, which eats into profits and cash flow. I will make exceptions if we find superstars with a lot of experience, however. Those are the type of team members we will bring in as fast as we can.

I may have a pool of potential hires, but I generally wait as long as I can before offering positions to them—except for good sales people. Usually that doesn't happen until my managers are screaming that they need more help. This only works for back office overhead, not in frontline sales, quality, or customer service.

Every person you hire adds to the complexity and the cost of operating your business, which is why I prefer to hire when there is an obvious need rather than hiring too soon. Still, unless your goal is to stay small and run a one-person shop, you will have to hire help for your business, and when you hire the right people for the right jobs, they can take your production and sales to new levels.

As the owner, you have to protect yourself and your business by creating a list of every potential position along with a summary of its purpose. This includes all that goes with each position, including job responsibilities, physical and educational requirements, and specific skillsets needed. Other costs and considerations include essential equipment and office furnishings, training programs, job goals, chain of command, salary range, and vacation and benefits offered.

Hiring for a rapidly growing business can be an overwhelming task, and extremely time-consuming. In the beginning, entrepreneurs can often handle several roles in the business, but when you reach a certain level, you need to bring in more people to keep the business growing.

I'm not a huge fan of bringing in human resource professionals early on to do my hiring. The other option would be to sign up with a recruiting service. Farming out the hiring process to professional recruiters may save you time, but it comes with a price tag. Usually, I will hire a headhunter initially to identify and recruit team members because they can target people with special skill sets more easily, and they also generally provide some sort of guarantees to replace their recruits who don't work out.

Recruiting services often charge fees equal to 20 to 30 percent of the salary of each hire. They usually find very well qualified people I never could have dug up. They will help you define the job and its responsibilities, recruit candidates, and conduct interviews to pare down the list. You will probably want to sit in on interviews with the most promising applicants, and definitely with the final two or three.

In these sessions, I always have to remind myself to resist hiring someone I like simply because we have a lot in common. I don't need another me—and neither do you. Entrepreneurs should hire those whose skills and experiences complement—and hopefully— exceed their own.

I'm a numbers guy, so I've got the financial aspects of my businesses pretty well in hand. Even so, I still have five other CPAs who help me keep track of everything and implement improvement. I don't know everything, and I can't do everything. An entrepreneur who can't delegate responsibilities won't be able to grow a business beyond a few employees. It is also important to listen and learn from your employees as the business grows.

And once your needs grow to more than a couple employees, you might need help in recruiting and hiring more. Fortunately, there are now many more resources available than when I started as an entrepreneur.

Back when Myrna and I were so busy growing our family as well as the nursing retirement centers and Pavestone, we didn't have online resources like Craigslist, Google, Glassdoor, Indeed, ZipRecruiter, CareerBuilder, and LinkedIn as recruiting tools. We depended more on placing ads in local newspapers and trade journals, word-of-mouth referrals, and recommendations from team members.

Myrna, who proved to be an excellent manager, hired most of our nursing retirement center employees and trained them. We had more than 2,400 in our 15 properties at the peak. With Pavestone, we reached nearly 2,700 employees in our 20 plants at one point.

I did the hiring at first, and then, as we grew, I used headhunters. With my current company, we still use the occasional headhunter, but most candidates come from online companies or web searches.

We believe strongly in hiring people with college degrees who are willing to keep learning and expanding their knowledge base. Yet we also will consider candidates who may not have college educations but who have great experience in the logistics industry or specialized skills for the positions we are filling. I've been happy to pay for top talent to get their MBAs in order to help them grow with my company.

Bedrock is a service business, and like any banking or accounting firm, we expect all of our people to be skilled in building customer relations, self-motivated, and creative in finding new business opportunities.

Many of our hires are for sales positions in which the team members contact trucking companies and shippers nationwide, trying to match up truckers in need of cargo and shippers in search of economical transportation for their goods. It is a direct sales operation that requires high levels of energy and self-motivation. We try to find loads and make money for the truckers who might otherwise be traveling back home empty, and we try to help shippers find good deals for deliveries and reliable service.

HIRING STRATEGIES

Like every employer, my companies always look for reliable, experienced people with skills and knowledge specific to the job openings we have. It can be challenging, however, because of federal and state laws that prohibit asking questions regarding personal matters, arrest records, health issues, and job injuries.

In my businesses, the bad hires have usually been people who overstated their abilities or exaggerated their skills during the application process. They may get hired by doing that, but they can't hide for long. Everyone's performance is measured, or should be, and if a hire does not live up to or exceed the expectations, well, that person won't be around long.

It's the difference between being a true professional and being a pretender. I've never had a problem firing someone who didn't live up to expectations. Now, I have more compassion if someone is a good person in the wrong job due to poor career choices. If I can direct someone worthy of trust into a job that is more suitable, whether inside or outside our companies, I will do that whenever possible.

In our nursing retirement centers, Myrna has handled terminations in a straightforward manner by telling employees the truth, as she was doing them a favor in the long run. She would convince them that leaving was their best option so they could work somewhere that suited them better.

It's tough for me to terminate people even when I know it should be done. I tend to believe in my father's old-school philosophy, "If you can't say anything nice, don't say anything at all."

I'm still not the greatest at cracking down on employees who aren't performing up to expectations. My son and daughters share that reticence. Myrna has worked with us to be straightforward and to position it as trying to help the employee find a better path.

I understand that sometimes people take jobs without really considering the long-term implications, and whether this is really a position that makes the best use of their talents and interests. If someone isn't happy in the job, or doesn't perform up to standards, I believe it's best for them to move on because they can take it as a wake-up call to find a better position for themselves.

I'm sure you've heard many people say that getting fired from a job earlier in their careers was the best thing that could have happened to them, and I think that's true in many cases.

TEAM MEMBERS WITH FAMILY TIES

People often ask if any of our kids work for our companies, but Myrna and I seem to have raised a family of entrepreneurs who have all chosen their own paths. None of them have wanted to work for our businesses and that's okay with us. We probably would have welcomed them if they'd wanted to join us, but my perception is that all of our kids thought they could create more interesting careers and businesses than the ones that we've had. It's not hard to understand why nursing retirement centers, paving stones, and trucking logistics didn't seem sexy to them, but to each his own, or her own.

We have had many fathers and sons working within our companies, and maybe even spouses and some mothers and daughters over the years. Many families have had successful businesses with relatives on the payroll, of course, but I am proud of our kids, now adults, for wanting to follow their own paths. That's not to say that Myrna and I haven't helped their enterprises at times, and we've always been available to offer our advice—sometimes more than they want—but usually to spare them from making the same mistakes we have made.

Some companies have anti-nepotism policies against hiring family members. Employees may feel it is hard to advance if the owner's children or relatives are set up to take over a position. The concern is that other employees might be tempted to think those family members get favored treatment, which is understandable.

Even more businesses ban employees from dating or marrying. I'm not one to lay down edicts like that, especially considering the fact that Myrna and I worked so closely together in the PeopleCare business for many years. We had our disagreements, certainly, but we never let "work problems" hurt our relationship. All I can say is that we are still married!

Now, at Pavestone, we did have a policy that said supervisors shouldn't date their employees. The truth is, you can't really tell people they aren't allowed to fall in love. One day, two employees who'd each worked for us for several years came in and announced that one of them had to quit because they were getting married.

I didn't know they'd been dating. They'd kept it quiet, and they were both valued members of our team. I congratulated them and said they were both welcome to continue working for us. They married and stayed with Pavestone, and we all lived happily ever after. One of them recently retired, and the other is now my longest-serving employee at thirty-five years! They were fantastic members of our team with very different skillsets, so it worked out.

FINDING THE RIGHT PEOPLE WITH THE RIGHT SKILLS FOR THE RIGHT POSITIONS

You might find it interesting to learn that one of the team-building strategies we created to keep our heads above water at Pavestone's plants was to hire a crew of U.S. Navy veterans who'd earned their stripes underwater—in nuclear submarines. Now that may seem like a curious move at first. After all, what do concrete product manufacturing plants have in common with nuclear submarines?

"A very challenging environment for their machinery and its maintenance," says Bill Karau, whom I hired, and who today still serves as a Pavestone senior vice president in Dallas.

We brought Bill aboard Pavestone in 2004, when demand for our landscape products was nearing its peak. Our sales were approaching $300 million. We were just completing our fifteenth new plant in Colorado Springs and building our sixteenth in Las Vegas when we recruited Bill to become our chief operations officer.

He was definitely the right guy for the right job at the right time. He is very much a processes guy with an engineer's mind for efficiency and technical mastery. We made a good team because our skillsets complemented each other.

Believe me, I do not want to be the smartest guy in my company's conference rooms. I have always strived to hire people who knew more than I did about their particular areas of specialization so that I could turn them loose and watch them succeed. My hope is that they can teach me a thing or two in the process to make me a better technician, a better person, and a better entrepreneur.

That is an important point for every entrepreneur to understand. While we tend to be hard-charging, self-confident, and goal-oriented, we shouldn't limit ourselves with a "my-way-or-the-highway" mentality. We should build teams in which every employee has skills and knowledge and experiences that make us all better and smarter at our jobs.

Bill has teased me for being a "swashbuckler" because even though I am very much a numbers guy, I tended to be willing to make bold and often high-risk moves if I think they can boost growth in my businesses. I certainly didn't need anyone egging me on to take on greater risks to increase profits. Instead, Bill helped improve and refine processes in our manufacturing plants to achieve the same goal.

At the time, the COO was responsible for manufacturing, sourcing, engineering, product development, administration, and safety. Bill was uniquely qualified because his résumé began with an architectural engineering degree and an MBA from the University of Texas, and included five years of service as an officer on U.S. Navy nuclear submarines. He followed that up with nearly five years as a process engineer, project manager, and financial analyst in the semiconductor industry with Motorola, and then nearly six years with McKinsey, working with major corporations to improve their management practices.

Bill Karau was a big hire for Pavestone at that point. We had been building plants across the country to meet the demand for our landscaping products and we still couldn't keep up with all the orders. We knew that level of demand would not last forever, so rather than keep building concrete plants, we needed to focus on improving productivity with the existing manufacturing facilities.

In short, we needed to generate more production out of our equipment by making it more efficient and more reliable. One of our biggest challenges was maintenance of our machinery in the concrete plants, due to all of the gritty dust that wears on equipment. Sand, gravel, and cement are highly abrasive, and they build up on and within machines. Breakdowns are common and it takes massive amounts of work to keep up with the maintenance and repairs.

That is where Bill's experience in nuclear submarines came into play. It's difficult to think of a more challenging environment for reliability in maintaining machinery than a nuclear submarine operating under enormous pressure deep in the saltwater seas of the world. Crews aboard Navy subs are trained to maintain and operate their equipment properly and professionally because if things go wrong, the entire crew may find itself in an extremely dangerous situation.

When equipment fails deep in the ocean, there is a very small window for repairs. Death can come within seconds. For that reason, no shortcuts or quick fixes are allowed.

"Submariners are trained to keep complex machines operating without a bunch of bubblegum and bailing wire holding it together," Bill says.

Technical competence and operational efficiencies are not goals, they are requirements in the submariner culture, and that was what we wanted to instill in Pavestone plants. We had built plants across the country because you can't ship landscape paving stones very efficiently for very far due to their weight and bulk.

So instead of one large plant in a central location, we had to have smaller facilities and smaller staffs in each. The value of a load of pavestone is only about $2,000, so it can easily add 15 to 25 percent in freight costs if you have to truck it over 150 or 200 miles. So, in a perfect world you will need a plant every 300 or 400 miles.

"That meant you couldn't have a white-collar computer geek doing administrative work and a bunch of blue-collar guys turning wrenches in every plant. You have to find guys who can manage a sophisticated program and fix things, too—and those are hard to find," Bill says.

Except in the U.S. Navy's submarine program. Or, more accurately, except for those who were veterans of that program and looking for work. Bill sought out other nuclear submariners, and we ended up hiring a half dozen or so Navy vets.

"Their skills don't apply to every area but when it came to turning small rocks into big rocks, a hell of a lot was directly linked," Bill notes. "When it comes to maintaining equipment and operating it efficiently and effectively, so you don't end up in a hostile environment, your average submariner is very good at that."

During his previous stint with Motorola, Bill had discovered after hiring former Navy friends that there were benefits to hiring a group of people with similar backgrounds and experience. It allowed for a "plug and play culture," as Bill called it, in which the new hires could step in and very quickly help implement positive change.

The former submariners shared a common language, which helped us do a rapid upgrade without a lot of groping around and searching for a consensus. We basically took a set of operational values from one culture and imported it into another.

Now, as any business leader can tell you, when you introduce an entire set of employees from one culture into another, there is bound to be some friction between them and the employees, who were not Navy veterans, but had more seniority in the company. Some of our longer-term people complained that when we brought in a half-dozen or so Navy veterans, they were made to feel like outsiders.

One or two even complained that it felt like there had been a hostile takeover. One of the older Pavestone veterans was quoted as saying, "What the hell do I know about making concrete? I've never even been in a submarine!"

Bill's job was to get everyone working together as quickly as possible, and I wasn't paying him to stroke egos and win the Mr. Congeniality Award. Or, as he says, "I didn't come to Pavestone to take us all on a mission of joint discovery. We were doing it the Navy way not because it is the best way or the only way, but because it is a good way that I knew would work."

Looking back to his first few years with Pavestone, Bill admits that he may have been so mission-focused that he fell back into old Navy habits and may have been too forceful for the civilian workplace.

"If you don't preface directives to employees with a 'please' and use good manners, even small things can be misinterpreted. I wasn't particularly good at making that transition even though I'd been out of the Navy for ten years and had worked for very progressive companies. Some of my old habits died hard."

Bill and his team led our efforts to make our equipment more reliable and efficient. This was an expensive process that involved bringing in some high-dollar people to repair machinery that had broken down repeatedly.

We also implemented a computerized maintenance management system (CMM). Essentially, we put together a small cadre of managers and corporate staffers, including one responsible for building a national maintenance program and another responsible for national process engineering and lab work to develop those processes.

Our goal was to hire people who could help us get more uniformity and consistent quality pushed out to the plants, and thereby build accountability into the system. Bill brought in another submariner who had been his division chief petty officer in the Navy. In fact, he had to talk the guy into retiring so we could bring him to Pavestone.

"I was his boss on the boat, when he joined the company, but I learned more about submarining from him than he did from me," Bill says.

That brings up a key point I want to make about team building for your business. My hiring of these military veterans did not mean that the instituting of a strict command and control, top-down, organizational structure. Bill is a very confident and no-nonsense guy, but he notes that people often have the wrong impression of how things really work on a submarine.

There is a chain of command, but competence is respected at all levels. The same should hold true in any business. If you are careful about hiring and training your team members, you should be willing to listen to them and defer to them if they are right and you are wrong, or if they have a better idea about how to do their jobs.

"It really isn't the case that you have a commander of the ship and everyone else is a robot," Bill explains. "It just doesn't work like that. Like all leaders, after a time I realized that I need to use my ears more than my mouth so that I could learn from my team."

He noted that in the U.S. Navy, a higher-ranking officer will give direct orders without saying please and thank you, but he will also listen and even defer to more experienced or more knowledgeable subordinates. The goal is to get it right every time while working for the overall team goals.

"The nuclear Navy, in particular, has very good principles that I saw work in the semiconductor industry, too," he says. "They have a concept or principle called 'forceful backup,' which means if your superior tells you to do something that is procedurally incorrect, you do *not* do it. Instead, you respectfully say, 'Sir, procedure bars us from doing what you just ordered me to do.'"

Bill was running a drill just three months into his first stint as a submarine officer when he ordered his electrical operator to do something, and the more experienced subordinate refused.

This was not insubordination. It was the correct response to an incorrect order.

"People often don't understand that it really isn't about command-and-control leadership as much as they might think," he said. "In this case, I made a greenhorn mistake when I ordered him to shift to a half power lineup. And even though I was his boss and the guy who wrote his job evaluations, he did not hesitate to refuse to follow that order."

Bill reports that after this incident, his captain supported the subordinate's response by noting to him, "You have a good command presence and you are forceful in giving orders and that is good, but you don't know what the hell you are doing."

The lesson here is that if you respect the hard-earned competence of your best team members, they might save your bacon. If you don't, they might not.

HOW TO KEEP GOOD PEOPLE

I tend to be overgenerous and overly accessible to my employees because I think of them as family. For example, I've always had an open-door policy where anyone could come to me at any time to make suggestions or to express concerns. That did not always sit well with my managers, who thought *they* should serve as gatekeepers and screeners. Some of them were threatened by employees who would come directly to me, so I had to be diplomatic about that!

I think it's better to be approachable. It's my business and my risk, and I want to know what is going on. When Myrna was running our nursing retirement centers, she'd spend a lot of time walking through them and making herself available to staff members and our clients. People call it MBWA (Management By Walking Around.) She knew the business so well that she wasn't afraid to hear suggestions and to make them, too.

Her focus was always on giving our residents the highest quality of care in their daily life, and the staff picked up on that from her example. She also understood that often there isn't time to go through a chain of command in situations when a resident's health and welfare is endangered.

COMPENSATION CONCERNS

Compensating your people well and letting them know they are appreciated is another important matter. When you are hiring for special skill sets like veteran engineers, medical professionals, and IT wizards, you have to be competitive in compensation. They expect to be paid the market rates and to have benefit packages reflective of their value in the marketplace.

Beyond that, you also have to take into consideration the personality types you are dealing with. As Bill notes, when you are hiring people for their technical competence in manufacturing operations and similar enterprises, they tend to have a more objective frame for being valued.

These are not touchy-feely, squishy type of people. While other types may need reassurance and encouragement, those with more of an engineering mindset often could care less about being patted on the back by their supervisors. In fact, they may be suspicious of that sort of thing.

"High horsepower operations people are more accomplishment oriented," Bill says. "They get frustrated if they don't feel they are fully engaged and making a significant contribution. They know when they are killing it on the job and they don't need to be told that—especially by someone who doesn't understand their worth.

The key to managing these employees is to give them opportunities to make significant changes. Let them make decisions and even make mistakes. Let them leverage what they know to turn something bad into good or something good into great."

Our Bedrock sales team members typically are not long out of school or in their early thirties with experience working on sales commissions. Our sales staff is very young. It's an intense job, but the rewards can be significant. Most start with a base salary, but they can double or triple it with bonus commissions, which is pretty good for someone a few years out of university.

We offer them personal time starting out, but honestly, they rarely take all of those days. Most of them are very competitive and eager to make as much as they can in commissions, so they find the job addictive. Sometimes we have to suggest they take a few days off so they don't burn out. As an additional incentive, they know that we are a growing organization that promotes from within, so they see there is room to advance up the ladder.

When you think of your employees as team members who follow the company's values and mission while pursuing both their individual and our business goals, it creates a bond that hopefully elevates your relationship beyond the standard transactional workplace. That's always been my goal. I strive to build a trusting and mutually supportive environment. I want to be able to depend on my people and I want them to know that I will be there for them. I sincerely want them to do well in their careers and their lives.

I have been blessed with a wonderful wife and family. I want my employees to feel blessed in their lives, too. If someone who has done good work for our company needs help for a personal matter,

I do my best to help them out any way I can because I want our best people to feel appreciated and supported.

We had a wonderful Pavestone manager who was stricken with cancer. He had a wife and three beautiful children, and we did everything we could to help him during his fight. Sadly, we lost him, but I had let him know that his family would be taken care of, and I followed through by paying off their mortgage so his wife could keep their home for raising their kids.

We helped another of our employee families adopt a child when they couldn't have their own. They still send us photos of graduations and other special occasions, which warms our hearts.

OPEN LINES OF COMMUNICATION

As much as I strive to create a family atmosphere within my companies, that doesn't mean I am willing to accept poor performances that negatively impact our bottom line or put our customer relationships at risk. Entrepreneurs have to set standards of operation and performance and then communicate openly with their employees when they are not meeting those expectations. The key is open and constant communication that run both ways, and throughout the entire organization.

Along with the monthly profit and loss reviews with top managers, Pavestone held Monday morning conference calls that weren't exactly popular but proved to be highly effective. These calls were necessitated by the challenges that came with the highly competitive and very seasonal market for our landscaping products.

Our biggest customers were Walmart and Home Depot, and every spring their landscaping departments were flooded with customers looking for ways to beautify their properties. This was true even in parts of the country that stay warm year-round. It was just a spring thing, the time of year when everyone wanted to whip their yards into shape.

As you can imagine, this creates a huge spike in demand for landscape materials. Our job at Pavestone was to have the right products already stockpiled and available each spring to meet that demand for our customers so they could provide it to their own customers.

The big challenge we faced involved getting our heavy concrete products delivered to Home Depot and Walmart stores. Pavestone's internal freight capacity was usually overwhelmed each spring, even with our own fleet of 300 tractor trailers. So, we had to hire hundreds of more independent truckers to get our product to the stores on time. Of course, many other seasonal product makers—yard mulch and lumber, for example—were also trying to ship goods to their customers, which meant there was always a feeding frenzy for flatbed trucks that drove up freight prices.

During Pavestone's rapid growth in the early 2000s, we had numerous instances in which loads were shipped short or not on time. To deal with this challenge, we held conference calls each Monday morning with all our sixteen plant managers.

We went through every order that had gone wrong at every plant, so things often got tense.

"It could be brutal," Bill recalls. "I wasn't browbeating people, but everyone had to answer questions on why their loads were late with all of the GMs on the call. It was peer pressure. You just shine daylight on an issue so everyone knows about it."

While these calls could be painful for those who'd missed the mark, the open conversation about common challenges often sparked helpful conversations on how freight problems could be alleviated, and often that involved cooperative efforts between plants to help each other out.

People want to do well. Our guy in Kansas City didn't want to let down our people in Atlanta. We were all trying to satisfy the same customer, so these calls forcing problems into the daylight helped us learn from each other.

Bill noted that the legendary Admiral Hyman G. Rickover, known as the father of the nuclear Navy and a stickler on training and quality control, published technical bulletins listing mistakes and how they happened aboard nuclear submarines. Everyone onboard had to read and sign off on the bulletins to ensure that they learned from those mistakes.

It was about accepting responsibility for our own failures, so we got better, and that's what we were doing at Pavestone. We flogged ourselves to death for an hour and a half on those calls and suffered through it together so we would learn to do better. No one wanted to be the heel or the fool. They all wanted to perform. These calls were much better than talking to people individually because everyone learned from each other's mistakes. And no one person had to be the bad guy.

At Bedrock, we have weekly video conference calls, called "team huddles," with every office and its staff early in the morning. These are not long meetings because we want our salespeople working the phones with clients or potential clients as much as possible. We only take five to eight minutes for these huddles. Every office and team leader has a representative report on what they are doing and what they are hearing from the field. It helps us all get a feel for the market overall and the industry climate.

The huddle conferences are also a method for holding people accountable. If a guy reports he is working on filling ten or twenty truckloads one day, but the next day says it fell through, we want to know why. You have to be wary of guys who talk a big game, but don't produce. We keep the lines of communication open, both ways, and let them know we are paying attention. We are quick to give them credit when they do well, and we are just as quick to question them if their performance isn't up to our expectations.

I consider our employees to be our partners in the business. We all have a personal stake in our mutual success.

My concern for our employees extends to their health, too. I won't hire smokers or recreational drug users if they are that self-destructive with their own lives. We have always offered to help smokers find ways to break that habit so they can continue to work with us. My philosophy is that if people refuse to look after their own health, I can't trust them to do what's best on the job for our customers and colleagues.

Building trusting relationships and partnerships with employees is essential, and that's why I take it so seriously.

Sometimes I get a little carried away, at least according to my kids. I used to send out free subscriptions to health magazines or emails about healthy lifestyles. One day, my son Kirby sent me an email with the heading "100 reasons you should drink a lot of water." He knows that I'm a big advocate of drinking water throughout the day.

I looked through the first twenty or so reasons and they were all sensible enough. Then I got a call and didn't take the time to look through all 100 reasons before forwarding the email to all of our 2,700 employees at the time.

And I do mean *all* of our employees! It was a mass email from the chairman, so of course everyone thought they should open it and read all the way through it.

As it happened, we had just hired a new human resources director and a few minutes after I sent that email, he came barging into my office. I could tell he was nervous about something as he stood there looking at me with a mix of fear and concern.

"Hi, what's going on?" I said.

"Bob, you *really* can't be sending out emails like the one you just sent out to everyone in the company," he said.

"You mean the one about drinking plenty of water? What's wrong with that?" I asked laughing.

"Open it up," he said.

I opened the email.

"Now scroll through all the way to the hundredth reason," he instructed.

I scrolled all the way to the end, and to my horror, the final reason was a photo of a woman with the largest chest I'd ever seen, barely contained in a bikini top, chugging a bottle of water.

It was beyond inappropriate! I immediately sent out another mass email as an apology, and I later had a few choice words with my son, who couldn't stop laughing during the entire lecture.

"Read everything, Dad!"

Chapter Six

BUSINESS SUDOKU, DRIVING, AND MANAGING GROWTH

My son-in-law has described Bedrock Logistics as my "giant sudoku game." I can't disagree much with that. My goal is to grow this one-stop matchmaking service for shippers with goods and truckers with capacity into a $500 million business in the next few years.

In 2012, its first year as an independent company, Bedrock's revenues were $13 million, and we expect to surpass $200 million in 2022 with more than 70,000 deliveries. That will require getting every aspect of the business in sync.

Only half of all the new businesses started survive beyond the five-year mark. Only a third are still around after ten years. To grow a start-up into a successful and enduring business, all the numbers need to line up, and as my son-in-law noted, the key is also playing my favorite puzzle game.

Sudoku is a logic-based "brain game" in which you must fill a nine-by-nine grid consisting of eighty-one squares, using numbers ranging from one to nine. The grid is divided into nine sub-grids consisting of nine squares each. The catch is that you may use each number only once per horizontal and vertical line and within each of the nine sub-grids.

I learned about the game while watching Myrna working on some puzzles. My wife tried to get me interested in doing them, too. She thought sudoku would be right up my alley, given my penchant for numbers-crunching.

I resisted initially, thinking it would be a waste of time. But every once in a while, she would ask for help, and before I knew it, I was hooked. Now, I play usually once a day when I am on my exercise bike. On flights, we even look for extra copies of the same newspaper so we can race each other on the sudoku puzzles published.

I buy sudoku books with the most challenging puzzles to stay sharp and hone my skills. I'd been playing for a year or so before I discovered that sudoku is known to be popular with entrepreneurs around the world. That makes sense. Business creators usually have the right skillsets for this game, and in both sudoku and business, success comes only when all the numbers are in alignment.

It's also true that with these puzzles and with a growing. a business, you have to pay attention to both the details and the overall big picture. That is how you make sure the company is on track and aligned with your goals for it.

My friend Jim, who led two Fortune 500 companies, is a sudoku fan too, and he gets the connection. "Like most entrepreneurs and business leaders, Bob is always checking one box against another so at the end of the day, every part of the business works in sync and it all comes together," he said.

At least once a day, sometimes more often, I get on my computer and check the numbers on the Key Performance Indicators (KPI) for Bedrock Logistics and any other projects I have going on.

Choosing the appropriate KPIs for your business is like picking the right numbers for a sudoku puzzle. To be successful, the numbers have to work. These key indicators help you determine where improvements can be made by your team members, processes, and the overall business.

They also provide quantifiable information that you can use to guide your business decisions and resource allocation. They are useful in determining the performance levels of your team members and divisions, as well, so you know where to pat backs and where to kick butts, figuratively speaking, of course.

At Bedrock, we've used KPIs to set sales objectives and determine which sales staff members are performing at the highest levels, which results in increased sales and productivity.

Our sales VP Andrew says he finds the KPI of margin per load helpful in motivating members of the sales team. "I tell them this metric is about them making more money. And how the mechanics work!"

Using this KPI has worked well for us. In 2015, our margin per load was half of what we are achieving now. Earning increases like that motivate salespeople in a big way, while also helping the business grow.

Overall, having well-defined key performance indicators improves our ability to make business decisions that are in sync with our goals while also working as a budget tool to contain costs.

BETTER, FASTER, CHEAPER

If well chosen, your KPIs will tell you whether your business is growing at the desired rate. You will also get a reading on the efficiency of your processes and people. Our KPIs provide a measure of the speed, quality, and cost of key processes and the specific employee actions that produce our desired results.

For example, speed—the time it takes to deliver or produce a product or service—is a key performance indicator in most businesses because your goal should be to always do your job better, faster, and cheaper. Time, then, is a driver of efficiency and customer satisfaction, and measuring it helps you streamline your production and manufacturing processes.

Your company's KPIs should offer you a clear understanding of what is working and what isn't. This critical information lets you know what adjustments have to be made to keep growing and going with the business.

I made sure our top people know what the expectations for each KPI are, and they can check to see where they stand on those expectations and in relation to each other. This is a measure to achieve our goal of constant improvement.

CHOOSING THE KPIS THAT WORK FOR YOUR BUSINESS

Key performance indicators will vary from business to business, and even department to department, but generally they measure the performance of each important business outcome. They are aligned with your most important objectives, so you should be careful in deciding what to track. The two most important KPIs in most enterprises are usually:

1. How much money do we have today and/or what is our available line of credit? (You don't ever want to run out of money!)

2. What were our total sales, number of orders, numbers on our product shipments yesterday (or today)?

Also, simply tracking net profits doesn't tell you which lines are performing the best, so a KPI that measures percentage gross margin by product is more effective because it tracks profits from each product line. Your low performing products have nowhere to hide.

The wide range of KPIs differ based on the goals of the business, your requirements, and other outcomes you select. The challenge is to choose the right performance measures for the specific needs of your business and its various divisions and departments.

I've spent many hours choosing the most useful and relevant performance indicators for various departments and their needs. I have a knack for numbers and statistics, but I have to keep in mind that my employees have their own skillsets, which may not be the same as mine. So, one of my goals is to make sure the KPIs given them are those they can readily grasp and understand.

I also look for those performance measures that can be applied to see where we stand in relation to both short-term and long-term goals on a daily, weekly, and monthly basis, if possible.

There are several factors to consider when choosing the key performance indicators for your business. First of all, you have to know what you want to achieve in terms of your business goals. I set very specific and quantifiable goals for improvements in performance, production, and profits by identifying a specific percentage within a specific amount of time, such as a 25 percent increase in the next 12 months.

The most common key measures for financial performance include units sold daily, net profit, net profit margin, percent gross profit margin, revenue growth rate, return on investment, return on assets, return on equity, working capital ratio, operational expense ratio, price-earnings ratio, and operating profit margin.

Although the KPIs listed above are important, your KPI's shouldn't be limited to financial performance. For example, at Pavestone, we were also concerned with the performance of our operations. Key performance indicators there include overall equipment effectiveness, time to market, project cost variance, and quality index.

To give you a real-world example, when we focused on the Overall Equipment Effectiveness (OEE) at our Pavestone plants as a KPI, we quickly learned that we needed to upgrade our maintenance for all of our manufacturing machinery. We then made a major investment in our new maintenance program, and we recouped that investment in about a year because of the resulting gains in productivity and a reduction in capital expenditures.

KPIs also can be applied to market evaluation for your business. Common measures there include market share, conversion rate, social networking footprint, cost per lead, page views, bounce rates, market growth rate, and search engine rankings.

Key performance indicators also can help you measure employee performance, which is particularly important if your company provides a service. KPI's commonly used in that area include revenue earned per employee, salary competitiveness ratio, and employee satisfaction index. In this arena, your key performance indicators can help manage staffing costs and improve performance.

As motivation, we have a giant screen TV on the wall of the office showing every truckload and where it is in relation to the delivery. We also have performance targets that reward outstanding employee performance with bonuses and perks.

SAFETY FIRST, THEN QUALITY, THEN QUANTITY

We also used KPIs to track safety first at our Pavestone plants, then we focused on quality and then quantity when looking at all the numbers and making decisions. You also should make sure your expenditures are always in line with your overall goals for the company.

To decide what your KPI's are for a business, you have to determine your desired outcomes and why they are important, how you measure progress, how you influence outcomes, who is responsible for them, how you know when you've achieved them, and how often you review progress towards each outcome.

If you have a goal of increasing sales for the year, which seems like a good idea to me, then you create a sales growth KPI. You define it by setting the percentage of increase you are seeking for the year. Define what results you expect if that happens, such as increased profits due to increased revenues measured in dollars spent. You can then set methods for achieving that goal, such as adding sales staff and increased marketing to motivate customers to buy more of your product or service.

Next, you put someone in charge of achieving this goal for sales growth. Your sales manager might be a likely candidate. And you tell him to review the KPI and its progress on a set schedule: daily, weekly, monthly.

I am known as something of a fanatic when it comes to using KPIs as a measure of performance. I track them relentlessly. In the early days of Pavestone, I had to do this by calling around to all the plants and getting the data from employees. Now, I can monitor them in real time with software and dashboards on my computer. I'm sure my employees are grateful I'm not calling them all the time.

We teach everyone on our team what the key performance indicators are and why they are significant to the company's growth. In each of our businesses, people soon understand that what is measured matters!

Sometimes, business leaders get carried away with this and put too much of a burden on their employees and even their customers. In some service industries like restaurants and automobile dealerships, customer satisfaction has become such a critical measure of performance that their customers are inundated with emails every day from places we've purchased goods or services.

As clients, we could spend our whole days filling out these customer satisfaction surveys. Some companies place way too much emphasis on them. I've heard of restaurant chains that dock their servers, and stores that fire sales staff, if they don't get customers to fill out the surveys or if they don't earn high enough scores.

A friend told me that the service department at a car dealership badgered him so much about filling out customer satisfaction surveys that he quit taking his car there. I don't think demanding that your customers carry that burden is a wise policy. My advice would be to actually talk with your best customers, meet with them informally, or call them on the phone and ask them yourself.

I know that isn't always possible in a high-volume service business like a restaurant chain or hotel chain, but having your managers ask them if they are satisfied seems like a better solution than emailed surveys or constant requests for feedback.

KPIS I'VE KNOWN AND LOVED

With each of my businesses, I've identified a primary KPI that is a main driver financially for the company. With our nursing retirement centers, the primary KPI was all about stats per patient per day. Running our PeopleCare Centers was similar to running a hotel in that way. If you have empty beds, then you are losing revenue. So, a primary performance measure we looked at each morning was to check our occupancy rate with a daily census report.

We would call each of our properties to find out how many beds were vacant. If we weren't full, Myrna and I wanted to know why. *Are our residents leaving because they aren't happy? Are the meals not good? Is there a flaw in our customer service?*

Now, at the time, the average occupancy rate for nursing retirement centers in the state of Texas was 80 percent, but we often had waiting lists because our facilities were full, so we must have been doing something right!

We didn't take smokers because we didn't allow smoking in any of our centers. We wanted to improve their life enrichment and surroundings. And with our daily check of our primary KPI, we made sure we continued to stay on a positive track.

With Pavestone, our primary KPI was all about looking at the cost per equivalent square foot of raw materials (sand, rock, cement), labor hours, freight, and overhead. We would compare them daily, weekly, and monthly, ranking all the plants so each manager could make his own decisions on how to keep us competitive. Being the number-one plant for the month or year is obviously better than being number three or eighteen.

Our primary KPIs at Bedrock Logistics, our matchmaking service for shippers and truckers, include daily delivery reports or truckload shipments per day, daily revenue, and net revenue per person—the higher the better. If the net revenue per person is good, then the company is making money.

We have KPIs for our sales reps and the load amounts matched per person. We also measure the average margin percentage. After we struggled with our accounting systems, we put in better metrics for accounts receivable outstanding each day, and the aging of those accounts receivable.

GROWTH STRATEGIES

My specific growth strategies have been different with each business. Honestly, in my heart, I always thought I would grow my businesses and hang on to them all forever. But the reality is that I didn't do that with either the nursing retirement centers or Pavestone, and no one knows what will happen with Bedrock Logistics, either. I love working as an entrepreneur and creating careers and lifestyles for all the families our businesses support!

With the nursing retirement centers and Pavestone, the time came when I was ready to sell them. So, maybe I'm not really a "forever" kind of guy, except in my marriage, of course.

I've realized that what I truly enjoy doing with my companies is founding and developing them through the start-up and the growth stages until they reach a point where they are major players. Then, when the opportunity arises, pass them on to much larger billion-dollar companies that can use them as an exciting new addition to their family and provide all of their resources to continue to grow their platform to a whole new level.

Pavestone is a good example of this strategy. Over thirty-two years, I took it from start-up through scale-up. Thirty-two years may seem slow, but we had to build plants to keep growing, which ate up both time and money.

Once we had those huge customers on board, we drove growth also by adding more concrete product shapes like retaining walls, garden and patio edging materials, bagged landscaping rock, and marble, granite, and beach sand. Initially, those materials were bagged manually, but we sped up the process with automation and robots. We went from needing fifteen workers to just two or three guys in a high-capacity bagging plant.

Of course, any time you automate and add robots, then you need to hire engineers and maintenance people, but you get more educated employees who aren't doing backbreaking work, which is a benefit. The new product lines added 20 percent to our overall sales.

We were rocking right along with Pavestone, when in 2007, we received a substantial $540 million offer to sell to one of our largest competitors. That deal unfortunately fell through, no thanks to a government ruling. (I'll share the painful details in the next chapter.)

Then, like most businesses, we hit a wall during the 2008 financial crisis and the recession that followed. We went through several difficult years before regrouping and finally selling to another company four years later. They saw Pavestone and its manufacturing plants with our seventeen-hundred employees as a great platform for their company to quickly expand upon.

We'd built a platform business that allowed their company to make a major leap into the landscaping and home improvement industries by buying in rather than spending years and hundreds of millions building it themselves.

SCALING UP AND MOVING ON

Although it wasn't a conscious strategy, we essentially did the same thing with our PeopleCare Heritage Centers chain, buying low-performing operations and upgrading them to top-of-the-line facilities over the years. Once we had a really strong platform business, our chain of thirteen nursing and retirement centers in Texas had a total of twenty-two-hundred beds and twenty-four-hundred employees.

Again, it was a turnkey operation with innovative and top facilities that attracted buyout offers from large companies wanting to grow exponentially without investing many years in development.

We learned with both businesses that when you scale up to that "platform" level, larger companies are willing to pay more rather than building their own. I've seen that the leverage buyout companies, and the entire private equity industry looks for thriving businesses at that level because it instantly adds cash flow, and therefore so much value with current high multiples.

We sold to a public company that also wanted our expertise. They made Myrna a huge compensation offer to stay with the company management, but she was ready to move on. She felt her personal style of management wouldn't match up with that of a much larger company. Instead, she became a big source of help in human resources at Pavestone with her expertise in staff management and labor laws. She also threw herself into many philanthropic board positions, ending up as chairman of the Dallas Symphony Board. That was not a retirement job!

The cash-rich giants like Amazon, Google, and Facebook are always on the hunt for other businesses that have reached the platform stage. Amazon has been a corporate Pac-Man, spending billions on huge acquisitions including Whole Foods ($13.7 billion), Ring ($1.2 billion), and Zappos ($1.2 billion), to name just a few.

For such massively successful companies, it's easier to let someone else do all of the groundwork and scaling up rather than trying to grow their own business organically. That may or may not work. They are better off paying more and investing in others that have proven successful. That's why I tell younger and novice entrepreneurs to fight the temptation to sell off their companies too soon. Joe Byles, who is my partner in a solar venture that is just gearing up, has started several "green" companies and he made this mistake early on.

I'll let him tell you about it:

"Years ago, I had a company that grew plant materials to create 'green roofs' on homes and businesses. It was also for useful for growing plants in hanging baskets. It was still in the early stages when a $3 billion global corporation made me an offer for that business. I took the offer and received a healthy amount, but I have realized since that I sold that company way too early.

If I'd scaled it up and grown it for several more years, I could have sold it for much more. I won't make that mistake again."

GROWTH STRATEGIES

I'll tell you more about my partnership with Joe and our unique start-up in a later chapter. My growth strategies for that new company are much different for my other ongoing business, Bedrock Logistics.

Many businesses that ship freight can't afford to have a full-time staff who spends hours and hours on the phone trying to find a truck that will be in the right place at the right time to pick up a load and take it to the right place. So, we want to be the company they call when they get in a jam and need someone to find an empty trailer and a reliable trucker who can get the job done for them and their customers.

This high-tech twist on the trucking logistics field has been developing over the last ten years and it seems new leaps in software products are made nearly every week. There are already many major players in it, including Uber, so it has become highly competitive.

We experienced rapid growth from the start-up and actually outproduced our infrastructure so that we were making money, but some of our departments, accounting in particular, couldn't keep up. As our sales and operations VP Andrew Birkins says, "It was like we'd built a three-story house without floors."

When things slowed down, we had to shore things up, clean up, and become more efficient. Sometimes when you are growing so fast you don't have time to assess performances and operations. Once again, Andrew has a phrase for that: "It's like a relationship: You don't look at the bad stuff when everything is champagne and beers, but you do when it's fears and tears."

With a business like this, in which we sell a service rather than product, the primary way for driving growth is to hire more sales people, because each person can only handle so many trucks. We had 100 sales people at one point, and then dropped down as the market slowed due to international trade wars and other factors.

Even so, we try to stay ahead of the game by hiring people at a steady rate because the training program is challenging and the learning curve so steep.

Andrew Birkins notes that it takes three to four months before most of our new hires begin to pay for themselves and then nine months to a year before they are bringing in profits.

"We have to have the right people and sometimes you don't know you have them until they are here a while and go through all of the training," Andrew says. "Sometimes they don't work out and sometimes they become superstars who transcend the business."

At this stage, Bedrock's growth depends mostly on how fast we can find and bring in the right people and get them online, because most of them don't bring in enough to cover their salaries and training costs until after many months.

Believe me, it's more fun growing a business than scaling it back. If you are growing and going, the banks will look out for you and provide you cash when you need it, which makes life easier. Yet there is always a danger of growing too fast. The early warning sign for that is unhappy customers. If a shipper's goods aren't delivered on time, they'll let you know about it.

Retail stores in particular are under a lot of pressure to stock the shelves for their biggest sales periods, and if they can't get the products, they are not happy campers. Their standard line is, "If my customer wanted it delivered tomorrow, he would have ordered it tomorrow." Thanks to Amazon, people have the expectation that something ordered today often can be delivered today.

TECHNOLOGY CAN SPUR GROWTH

Bedrock Logistics is the most sophisticated business I've owned in terms of technology because the entire company is built around Transportation Management Systems (TMS) software used by our operations team who selects from tens of thousands of qualified carriers throughout North America.

We invest heavily in tech, but Andrew, who is more tech savvy than me, fears that to some degree, technology has been oversold. He believes that human intelligence and initiative can still trump the benefits of artificial intelligence.

Using technology as a growth tool can come with its own challenges. When we installed a state-of-the-art software system, it briefly threw us into a state of chaos. There always seem to be bugs that must be worked out in every software upgrade.

A few years ago, in one of our smaller divisions, we upgraded from QuickBooks to a more powerful Enterprise Resource Planning (ERP) and experienced several months of delays in our cashflow during the transition. Somehow, the new system had trouble with selecting the proper mailing addresses and most of our customer invoices were not being received by our customers. I had to put more cash into the company while we reentered a lot of information manually, which was a nightmare.

We also have developed our own smartphone app in hopes of growing our business with that technology. This entails an investment of a couple hundred thousand dollars, but if it brings in more customers and keeps us closely connected, we think it will be worth it.

Because our salespeople mostly work the phones to connect with shippers and truckers, they seldom see our customers, so this seemed like a natural step. We partnered with a company that tracks loads so our shipper clients can monitor trucks movement and location.

The app features the same technology used to track Uber cars. We want to be able to track every load so that our clients know when their shipments are being delivered. The app will allow shippers to set up accounts with Bedrock, hire us to handle their logistics of finding a truck, and then track it all the way.

GROWING BY SERVING CUSTOMER NEEDS

My favorite strategy for growing a business is to identify a customer's special needs that aren't being met and finding a way to fill those needs, which adds value for them and brings more profits for us. New software and customized apps for smartphones can help do just that.

If there is any business that relies on customer satisfaction, it is the nursing retirement center business. Residents of our homes had no problems letting us know, as they should, if they are unhappy with any aspect of their accommodations, meals, or daily care. Their families were also more than willing to offer their opinions.

At Pavestone, we grew product development by providing a variety of paver shapes, surfaces, styles, and colors, as well as making sure they were delivered when our customers needed them. We scaled up from an initial customer base that was mostly contractors and smaller landscaping and home improvement stores to the national, big-box stores, including two thousand Home Depots and five thousand Walmarts.

Those stores cater to the do-it-yourself landscaping and home repair market, which is enormous, but those shoppers mostly come in a big wave every spring, even in Southern states, with warm weather year-round. So, the stores have a very tight window for stocking their shelves and moving product from March until June or July.

We set ourselves apart from the competition by doing whatever it took to get our products to the retail stores on time. We made sure stores were stocked every weekend in the spring and organized as many as an extra thousand trucks on busy days. We made high-quality pavers, we delivered them on time, and we had a very good marketing program, and that kept our big-box customers coming back for more.

YOU CAN'T GIVE AWAY THE STORE

While product quality and reliable delivery were critical parts of growing Pavestone, pricing was always the biggest challenge. The big-box stores control so much of the market that they can make or break suppliers when it comes to pricing. Some of them will work with you, understanding that you have to make a profit to stay in business. Others will beat you to your knees.

We worked with those that would work with us and we walked away from those that made unreasonable demands. You can't give away the store. It's simple math. To stay in business and keep growing, you have to keep making a profit and positive cash flow! There is no point trying to break your own neck trying to serve customers who don't value your quality, service, or capacity to keep their customers happy.

The big-box stores would call in their competing suppliers for annual meetings and pit us against each other in the wholesale version of *Fight Club*. Our guys were fighters, but I always told them that our deals had to be win-win.

We actually "fired" a big-box retail customer that became unrealistically aggressive and eventually we made exclusive deals with other customers. The big-box chain that we walked away from, with the surprise advertising promotions and fees that we knew weren't efficient, began demanding that we pay more and more for their co-op promotions.

They managed to drive some suppliers into bankruptcy with their aggressive tactics, so we'd decided that we could no longer be subjected to their demands. We could afford to do that because we'd earned the loyalty and respect of their competitors, and as they really grew, we really grew.

GROWING PAINS

Reality check: While in the scaling-up phase, revenue growth is not a guarantee of continued success if your business is not also growing cashflow on its own.

Cashflow is actually the most important lifeline in every business—more important than profits. You can't count on credit during a phase that feeds on cash. Cash is your lifeline for survival at this stage, a time when many businesses fail.

Few entrepreneurs have pockets deep enough to carry a large emerging business and all of its needs in a competitive market, especially if they get blinded by early indications of success and start spending their reserves.

There is a major pitfall that can trap entrepreneurs steering a business through the growth stage. Too many of them get excited about revenue growth and the potential for profits, instead of focusing on cashflow. Please print this in your mind, if not on your forehead: "Cashflow is king!" We are constantly looking at what we can do at Bedrock to increase cashflow by billing faster and resolving issues with payments more quickly.

Lucky for you, and me, there is a KPI for that. It's called the Cash Conversion Cycle (CCC), and my advice is to never let it out of your sight as you grow your business from the start-up stage into the platform stage. The CCC tells you how much time it takes between the time your business spends a dollar—on inventory, marketing, hiring, training, or anything else—and the time you get a return on that expenditure in the form of cash or profit.

I check our cash report (the most important KPI) every day—sometimes, in the old days, two or three times a day. I want to know how much is coming in and how much is going out every day, and the projections for the days ahead.

Ideally, your growing business would generate cash before you need it, instead of spending it and then waiting for the return. That is why I am always looking for ways to improve cashflow by earning more than my businesses spend. It's common sense, but not all that commonly applied or possible in a growing business.

My wise farmer friend back in Canada put it this way: "A cash cow is better than a new barn." A successful businessman that I advise was weighing the fact that his business' market value was six times its EBITDA (Earnings Before Taxes, Interest, Depreciation, and Amortization.) I told him that having a business and its nice, consistent cashflow is often better than selling it and having to figure out what to do with that mountain of money—or worrying you've made the wrong choice!

Let's say his business is making $1 million EBITDA, so he could probably sell it for six to nine times EBITDA. But if he sells it, his $1 million in annual (and probably growing) EBITDA is gone forever.

Let's say he now has $7.5 million in the bank instead—not a bad problem to have! But he has to pay taxes on that money, say 33 percent (depending where you live), which leaves him with $5 million in the bank.

To get his $1 million in annual cashflow back, he will need to find a new investment that gives him an annual return of at least 20 percent, which is very difficult and highly unlikely for a guy who is used to operating his own business.

So think seriously about your options before you sell your cash cow. In most cases, you don't want to sell your cash cow unless you are worried about the health or longevity of your cow.

A lot of entrepreneurs don't invest all that wisely, which is why I think keeping cash flow is the better choice in many cases. It is difficult to make a strong return off investments and you have to pay taxes that reduce your investment earnings.

A sustainable business that generates a lot of cash can support a family for generations if it is wisely run. When I sell a business, I tend to quickly invest the money from it into another business, or two or three. That's what we crazy entrepreneurs do for fun.

Learning how to manage cash flow in a growing business is one of the greatest challenges for entrepreneurs. Believe me, I've screwed it up many times. Over the years, I've learned to get creative in cutting expenditures, increasing sales, and speeding up cash flow.

If you have good relationships with your vendors, you can work out ways to extend payment terms.

With Pavestone, the peak demand each spring meant that we had a huge infusion of cash, but then it slowed to a crawl in the fall. We couldn't just shut down our plants during the off-peak periods, so we convinced our suppliers to give us extended terms during the off-season so we could continue to run our plants, build inventory, and purchase raw materials year-round, and then we'd make it up to them when the cash was flowing again in the spring.

We negotiated a lot of winter extended-payment-term deals like that, and it allowed us to keep growing with efficient and consistent monthly plant production for us and our raw material suppliers, as well. A definite win-win.

Another option to boost cash flow is increasing prices, hiking up the volume of sales, cutting inventory, and reducing costs. Running lean in every division and department also helps by cutting down on wasted hours and raw materials, improving your processes, increasing your team's productivity, and boosting cash flow.

Other recommended strategies I've used or seen others use include working with customers to boost their cash flow so they can pay you on schedule, timing your billings to match your customer's payment cycles, sending out polite or even humorous alerts to customers regularly ahead of their bill due date, or rewarding customers for paying in advance or on time. A common incentive is a 2 percent discount for paying in ten days.

My training and experience as an accountant have proved valuable in growing companies, as long as I don't let my enthusiasm and high-risk tolerance blind me to the numbers on my spreadsheet. Every growth-stage business with 100 employees or even fewer needs a serious numbers cruncher standing watch and ready to revise goals based on facts, not hopes and dreams.

In general, it is obviously more efficient to self-fund growth rather than borrow money from lenders or bring in partners. At this stage in my career, I've had enough success that I can usually draw on my own funds. I've done that with Bedrock when we had problems collecting payments from customers, but I know that isn't possible for early entrepreneurs who have to look to others for funding in tight times.

OUTSIDE SOURCES OF FUNDS
FOR GROWTH-STAGE BUSINESSES

The good news is that a business that has been operating for several years with a developed market and proven track record of success has more options than a start-up when looking for capital. Bankers, especially, are a lot more inclined to make loans during the growth stages than during start-up.

Venture capital firms and private equity investors are also much more interested in a company at this stage, for better or for worse.

Like angel investors, venture capital firms invest in your business in exchange for ownership shares. They don't loan you money to be repaid. They want a percentage of your profits, or, more importantly, a percentage of the growth in value of your company after a certain period of time. And, they may push you to sell if the company's value increases. (Remember, six to nine times EBITDA!)

While individual angel investors tend to be individuals who are investors and willing to serve as mentors, the venture capitalists typically represent groups that invest in many businesses. Usually they specialize either in certain industries or industrial sectors, specific stages of a business, or geographic area.

Usually, the private equity groups will only talk to you after your business has been up and running for a few years. They have much deeper pockets, are more comfortable with risk, and are often seen as tougher-minded than angel investors.

In other words, they don't mess around. It's not personal with them, it's business. They are also harder to get to, and even harder to seal a deal with because they often are besieged with requests. If you have a friend, partner, or business associate on good terms with a venture capital or private equity firm and willing to provide an introduction, it certainly helps.

Because they are willing to take on more risk, they will often invest in smaller businesses that have difficulty attracting other types of investors. Understand that they are willing to take on more risk because they are looking for bigger returns. You may have heard the names of some of the largest venture capital firms, such as Sequoia Capital, Andreessen Horowitz, and Benchmark, which invest billions of dollars, but every major city has dozens of both venture capital and private equity firms.

Many were founded by titans of business. There are also smaller venture capital firms run by more familiar names, including wealthy performers and athletes. They, too, see the value of building even greater wealth by banking on entrepreneurs, but you can be assured that while the firm may have a celebrity name, it's likely run by people with degrees in law, accounting, and finance.

You really need to be careful and well-prepared to deal with venture capitalists or private equity. You would be smart to have your own team or list of professional lawyers, CPAs, and investment banker advisors lined up to help you deal with them. If investors are interested in your business, they will present you with a term sheet that covers all the important issues and serves as the foundation for your dealings with them, and theirs with you.

Be aware that the numbers they provide in your letter of intent are probably the best numbers you are ever going to see. And they are only going to come down from there as negotiations begin.

Probably the most important step in this stage is negotiating an agreed value for your business before the new capital is invested. The greater the value, the more control you keep as the majority owner. The venture capital firm has a different perspective on this. The investors will want a lower value because it means less risk and the potential for higher returns to them for their percentage of the company.

Key considerations in this negotiation include your track record as an entrepreneur, the market potential for your business, the existing assets of the company, including patents and technology, how far along the business is in terms of earnings, market share, public profile, and product development, investor interest, and the economic environment.

PRIVATE EQUITY FUNDING

Large private equity firms are funded by wealthy investors and institutions such as insurance companies, university endowments, and pension funds. They invest in a wide variety of businesses, but a limited number of them, as they are looking mostly for those with higher growth and potential value. They prefer established companies with opportunities for greater efficiencies and earnings.

There are some giant PE firms such as The Blackstone Group, The Carlyle Group, and Kohlberg Kravis Roberts, but there are hundreds of small local PE firms operating across the country.

Private equity can be a great source of funding in the right situations. Though, again, you have to be very aware that anytime you deal with private equity and venture capital, you are stepping into the shark-infested waters. As long as things are going the way they want them to go, you'll get along fine, but if you lose their confidence in any way, they will come after you and your company.

QUALITY OF EARNINGS

Most PE firms demand a "quality of earnings audit." The first time I heard this I thought, "No problem, our financials are accurate." However, I soon learned it has nothing to do with the "quality" or accuracy of your earnings, but it is really a search for flaws or clues to weak points in your operations they can use to justify a lower price than what they originally quoted in the term sheet or letter of intent. It's more like a search warrant and they are like the cops.

BE AWARE OF THE POTENTIAL DOWNSIDE
OF PRIVATE EQUITY PARTNERS

Every veteran entrepreneur has stories that reflect both the good and bad aspects of taking on private equity partners. You need to be aware that things can sour quickly in any high-stakes business relationship. There are sharks in these waters.

My friends and I often swap tales of finding ourselves among the sharks. Trisha Wilson, the owner-founder of a big hotel interior design firm, and I went through similar challenges with private equity investors around the same time. She brought in minority partners in the later years of her global interior design firm and came to regret it.

Throughout her career, Trisha had studiously avoided debt. She prided herself on that, but her investors were not as risk-averse when it came to finances.

"When push came to shove, there was more shoving than pushing," she recalled. "They kept trying to force me to recapitalize. They had a leveraged buyout and I paid it back quickly, but they kept wanting to borrow more. They said, 'We can pay it back,' but it was *me* paying it.

"I had no debt, but eventually they forced me into a sale. Now, it turned out that the sale was the best thing that could have happened, in retrospect, but these partners didn't like it whenever I said no, even though I still owned a majority of the company. They found ways to make my life miserable for a while."

Trisha and I spent many hours on the phone during that time because I was having similar problems with private equity partners at Pavestone, whom I mentioned earlier in the book. Initially, our partnership went well. They said they were in it for the long term, investing for generations. They claimed to be all about full transparency, but then they proved they had other ideas.

After eighteen months, they sold their entire company, including their share of Pavestone, which was a shock to us. I will tell you more about this in the next chapter. My quick advice is to just be aware that, unless you've protected yourself with things like first right of refusal or drag-along or tag-along clauses, your so-called friendly investors might try to steal your business right out from under you.

CUSTOMER-FUNDED GROWTH AS AN ALTERNATIVE TO VENTURE CAPITAL

Since going into debt or giving up a percentage of your business aren't the most appealing options, entrepreneurs have long searched for alternative methods for funding the initial phases and early growth of their businesses. Verne Harnish, a venture investor, and founder of the Entrepreneur's Organization, is among those who have endorsed customer-funded growth as a more appealing option.

John Mullins, an associate professor at the London School of Business, advocates this approach in his writings, noting that many founders of successful businesses have used various tactics to apply this model, including Dell, Costco, Airbnb, and Bangalore.

The five approaches to customer-funded businesses Mullins identifies include:

1. Pay-in-advance: Costco charges an annual membership fee to customers who pay to shop in its stores. These fees account for two-thirds of Costco's operating profits most years and they essentially funded its rapid growth into a major retailer. Michael Dell's business model was selling his P.C. direct to consumers, getting paid up front quickly, and then assembling the P.C. parts which he

bought under extended terms, basically eliminating the need for any working capital.

2. Matchmaker model: Creating a business like Airbnb doesn't need much startup money because it basically serves as a matchmaker between travelers in search of lodging and those looking for temporary renters.

3. Subscription models: Netflix is among the most successful companies that uses this form of customer-funding by charging a regular membership fee to grow its business.

4. Scarcity model: French online fashion retailer vente-privee.com began accepting only customers recommended by a member. It offers "flash sales" featuring limited items of top designer clothing and accessories at big discounts for brief periods.

5. Service-to-product model: The Danish founders of GoViral, which creates and distributes viral video campaigns, built a $97 million company from scratch without borrowing any venture capital. They funded it initially and then grew it by using the proceeds of each viral video campaign to fund the next.

Chapter Seven

WHEN BAD TIMES HIT, GET OVER IT AND GET ON WITH IT

*Blessed is the one who perseveres under trial because, hav-
ing stood the test, that person will receive the crown of
life that the Lord has promised to those who love him.*

James 1:12

The Bible has many quotes like the one above encouraging us to persevere through adversity. When members of our family deal with hard times, we aren't as poetic. We sum it up simply by telling each other, "G.O.I."

Get over it!

I know this seems like one of those things that is easy to say but much harder to do. I won't disagree with you there. My family and I know how difficult it can be to rise above challenges and move forward.

I've referred to some of our hardest times in earlier chapters. Myrna has suggested recently that angels were working behind the scenes during this awful stretch in which our business interests were blindsided and beaten by one crippling blow after the other.

I have to admit that my wife has a point, though at the time I would have argued that only the darkest of angels were at work. If you are skeptical that anything good can come from bad times, I don't blame you. But please read on, because I think you'll see that this is exactly what happened to me and my family.

I never would have made it through these trials without the love and support of my family and friends. Quite honestly, I became so distraught and depressed that I forgot to stop, smell the roses, and remember all of the good things in my life. I was ready to just give up at times, but I'm glad I didn't.

Entrepreneurs often take pride in their self-sufficiency. I certainly did. Yet never in my life have I been so grateful that I had forged and maintained mutually supportive and trusting relationships over the years. They served me well.

No, let me correct that. They saved my life.

BLINDSIDED, BS-ED, AND NEARLY BANKRUPTED

There were dark clouds massing over Wall Street as 2007 stumbled to an end, but high-flying Dallas seemed sheltered and far from the storm. Myrna and I certainly felt secure thanks to our family's entrepreneurial success on several fronts.

The year 2007 was our best at Pavestone and it didn't feel like the economy was headed for a rough patch. I felt little fear; in fact I was elated that the company I'd built from scratch and scaled up over a twenty-eight-year stretch was about to be sold. The buyer, a public company, had just announced in the *Wall Street Journal* their contract to buy Pavestone for $540 million.

At that agreed upon price, I could pay off the bank loans that had helped finance the company's growth. I'd still have about half left to pay taxes and to invest in new opportunities.

Come what may, I thought we would be recession-proof, and in a position to provide financial security for our children, grandchildren, and great-grandchildren.

I was like the hockey player standing on the ice and cheering as we scored the winning goal, only to have it recalled, and then get decked by a sucker punch from an opposing player.

I never saw it coming.

The shot that blindsided me came from Washington, D.C. and the offices of the United States Federal Trade Commission (FTC), which had reviewed the sale of Pavestone under provisions of the Hart-Scott-Rodino Antitrust Improvements Act of 1976.

The sale of Pavestone to Atlanta-based Oldcastle Architectural, owned by an Irish public company CRH, had seemed like a natural fit. We both made concrete paving stones and landscaping products. Our biggest customers were Walmart and Home Depot. Oldcastle had Lowe's and Kmart.

Any time two large competing companies decide to merge, Hart-Scot-Rodino and the FTC rules on whether combining them might create a business so dominant that it would have an unfair advantage in the market, which could lead to higher prices for consumers.

When the sale of Pavestone was announced, we filed all the paperwork with the FTC. We had received legal opinions that the regulative agency should have no problem with the sale. It seemed like a no-brainer because there were over a thousand concrete plants in the U.S., and so many other paving product competitors manufacturing similar products across the country.

Although Pavestone and Oldcastle were major players, together we represented only 15 percent of the nation's total concrete block business. We thought there would be no problem with the federal regulators. We cruised through the process all the way until the scheduled day of closing, thinking we were clear to do the deal. By that point, after Oldcastle's public announcement, most of our employees already felt that they were working for Oldcastle.

The morning of the closing we waited for confirmation that the $540 million was on the wire and then the bad news came: our attorneys called at about 8:30 a.m. and announced that the FTC had said to stop and wait because they wanted to do a second request for more information and investigate further.

After nine more months of interviews, legal fees, and reviews of every e-mail our company had ever sent, the FTC came back with its final ruling. The commission ruled that if Oldcastle bought our company, "It would reduce competition, quality, and innovation in the patio-brick and retaining-wall business, resulting in increased prices for consumers."

The FTC said that while Walmart, Home Depot, and Lowe's combined sold only 15 percent of concrete landscape products in the U.S., Oldcastle would have been positioned to provide 90 percent of them to three of the most dominant big-box stores.

None of us had foreseen that the federal regulators would look at the sale as a setup for a market monopoly because of the combined big-box store sales. Since when was 15 percent of national sales of a product considered a monopoly?

To this day, I don't know what was behind the FTC's decision. Some suspect that maybe one of the major players in our industry with a lot of political clout didn't want Pavestone and Oldcastle distribution logistics to become such a large supplier.

With one phone call, our customers could get truckloads of Pavestone products quickly delivered to thousands of stores! Our sin seemed to be more about our distribution capabilities than our unique manufacturing. Whatever happened, this ruling came at a terrible time and created the sort of nightmare that every entrepreneur fears. Maybe it was a badge of honor that the kids from Canada could create a behemoth that caused a monopoly in America.

I'd spent twenty-eight years building Pavestone from a start-up that catered to landscapers and builders into a complex business serving the big-box retail stores.

I'd developed systems for tracking every KPI and aspect of our operations because the margins are low on concrete pavers and they're very heavy and costly to ship. They are also prone to surface damage during transit unless special measures are taken. Our customers had a very narrow window to stock the pavers and sell them to do-it-yourselfers each spring.

Over the years, I thought I had everything covered. When the offer from Oldcastle came, I spent more than $20 million in those long nine months on legal fees and due diligence preparing the company for the sale. I intended to pay off the over $200 million in loan balances we invested building plants and working capital to scale up the company, including one that I'd personally guaranteed.

Then the deal collapsed. And then the economy was crumbling through 2008. All that we'd worked to build, for all those years, doing our best to treat our employees and customers well, was threatened, including the financial foundation I'd built for our children and grandchildren. Everything was threatened, despite all I'd done to protect it.

The worst was that I had no control over any of it. Entrepreneurs don't like being out of control. But the shots just kept coming.

The negative FTC ruling in 2009 and the recession that rocked our industry beginning in 2008 and got worse in the next few years were just the first of several surprise blows that left me reeling during this awful stretch. The collapse of the housing market caused a dramatic drop in sales, which made it impossible to find another buyer, especially one willing to pay a price similar to what we had negotiated with Oldcastle.

Our sales and the value of Pavestone were significantly dropping every month, it seemed. Then, in mid-2009, our creditors and bankers descended. We never missed a bank payment, but we had busted (as they say) a lot of bank covenants. Their lawyers demanded that the company quickly repay the loans that I had used to build our plants and grow the business.

When Pavestone was flourishing and cranking out a strong cash flow, I had personally guaranteed a $28 million piece of the loan.

This proved to be a huge mistake. A personal guarantee is a legal promise to use your personal assets to pay your business loan debts if your company fails to do so.

I asked the lenders to give me extended time at a higher interest rate, but they weren't about to do that with the global economy in ditch. The darkest hour came when we met with about twenty bank lawyers and just the two of our own at a big downtown bank conference table.

Every bank we dealt with was calling in loans totaling $200-plus million that I had taken out to grow Pavestone, even though we had never missed a payment. We had missed some of the covenants, however, as had many businesses hit by the Great Recession.

Even then, Pavestone was still profitable, though less than when the economy was booming. There was blood in the water and the sharks were circling. The same banks that had lined up to loan us money over the years were now bombarding us with threats and lecturing us on our lifestyle choices.

Myrna remembers feeling like a child being scolded at the dinner table. I was so angry, I could hardly speak. You learn who your true friends are in such times, and believe me, the list narrowed considerably. My wife also remembers a wealthy heiress approaching her at an event and saying, "Don't worry, honey, I'll still be your friend when you're poor."

Myrna said that conversation served as a lesson on how to pick her friends in the future.

In the meantime, one of our own lawyers was telling me that declaring bankruptcy was the best option—something I had no intention of doing. Then our lender's lawyers began threatening to seize our assets. "We can't take your home, under Texas homestead law, but we can take your furniture and you won't have anything left to sit on."

It was one of our own lawyers who delivered the line that hit us the hardest. He handed some forms to Myrna and said, "We'll need you to make a list of all your jewelry, cars, and other valuables, because they'll probably be coming after them."

We had never felt so desperate. The truth is we still had a considerable amount of valuable assets, but everywhere we turned, there seemed to be a banker or a lawyer threatening us or turning on us.

My friend Craig Hall, a well-known Dallas developer and entrepreneur who has made and lost fortunes, but always fought back to rebuild his business empire, recalls having dinner with Myrna and me in a restaurant during this dark time.

"I knew it was a low point for them and they looked very weary. I'd been in very similar situations, so I understood how they felt," Craig recalled in an interview for this book. "But Bob and Myrna rose from humble beginnings and built very successful businesses because they are by nature hard-working, optimistic, and happy people. They took this challenge one step at a time, hung in there, did what they had to do, and they survived because they have always been transparent and honorable people.

"They came from a small village and became successful in a larger city where they have made a difference in the lives of many others," Craig added. "I think others can learn from them that we all have the power to build lives of achievement. Each of us has that power, probably more than most realize."

What Craig says is true. Most people are stronger than they realize when they are truly tested. We eventually made it, but we had to take it day by day, step by step. And it was often painful. I'd made mistakes in my life, but I'd never felt like a failure.

There were moments in that crisis when I was afraid that would happen, that we would lose all that we'd worked so hard to build. Even worse, I did not ever want to let down my wife and my kids, or my employees and the charities and organizations we supported.

We felt especially bad when our son Kirby had to sell his valuable Triple-A baseball team, the Tacoma Rainiers, because I had helped put up collateral for his purchase and my creditors were after it.

Kirby was passionate about that team. They'd just won the Pacific Coast Triple-AAA league championship and fan enthusiasm was at an all-time high. Over his four years of ownership, our son worked so hard to take that franchise to a higher level. He helped secure a $40 million stadium renovation that transformed Tacoma's old baseball stadium into a modern ballpark, helped set new records for attendance, and attracted Fortune 500 sponsors.

The team's value had grown steadily under his leadership, even in the recession, and he still made a profit on the deal, but nothing like he would make if the sale hadn't been forced upon him. That is one of our biggest regrets from that period because I know how much Kirby enjoyed making that team successful.

The good news is that my son overcame his disappointment and in recent years has become very involved with our real estate ventures in California and Florida, where he is an integral part of the team.

AN ANGEL APPEARS

I am averse to declaring bankruptcy if it can be avoided, yet I know sometimes people have no choice but to take that option. I've never been one to walk away from a debt. I certainly fought it as hard as I could during this crisis. In 2009, I met with dozens of private equity firms and other lenders to raise capital. I might have failed in that fight, but another option opened up in January of 2010 when we received an offer from another family of entrepreneurs.

Known for their diverse holdings and generous philanthropy, the company offered to invest $100 million for half of Pavestone Company.

As desperate as we were, this was not an easy decision. No entrepreneur wants to give up half his company, but selling part of Pavestone was better than the alternative.

Our new partners pitched us well. They played to our sense of family, talking about this as a very long-term investment for them that would benefit all of our children and grandchildren. They seemed to have similar values and long-term goals, and we came to believe their offer was heaven-sent. We looked at this as a lifetime partnership based on what they told us. We had a family meeting, and everyone voted to proceed with the merger and partner with a new family office.

With their cash infusion, we were able to reduce Pavestone's debt and clean up the balance sheets. Things appeared to be looking up at that point, but it wasn't long before we began to have problems with our new partners.

We had gotten along fine with the investing family members, but the executive in charge of our partnership in Pavestone seemed to have a problem with our approach to business. He did not have the same style of management that our company was accustomed to.

Maybe it was a classic clash of business cultures. I tend to be an optimistic consensus builder who looks for win-wins in business deals. This guy was more of a bully and a dictator.

He did little to mask his contempt, including suggesting I resign from my own company!

Most of our Pavestone team had stayed with the company and remained loyal through all of the challenges of the previous years, even though many of them could have gone elsewhere.

Although he had no experience in the paver or landscaping supplies business, this rough-edged guy kept trying to tell me how to operate the company through his bullying tactics and verbal abuse.

I struggled with all of this turmoil in the company. For decades, Pavestone had been a healthy and fun place to work. We had many loyal employees who knew we were there for them if they needed us. I tried to treat everyone fairly and to show my appreciation for their hard work.

Now this outsider had stepped in and made life miserable for us. This is one of the dangers of bringing in outside investors, of course. Sure, some are benevolent and want everyone to succeed. That's how I feel about companies I've supported over the years.

Yet, there are those investors who want to micromanage and will try to take over your business or even sell it right out from under you. At one point, this executive threw out a low-ball offer to buy my half of the company—for $40 million. That was about $100 million less than it was worth at the time! (More on this to come.)

SKULLDUGGERY

Unfortunately, there was skullduggery that rocked the relationship and caused a great deal of distress as we realized our "angel" investors had a dark side. At one point, they claimed to have a potential buyer for Pavestone in Australia, but we later figured out this was simply a ruse to set us up for a bigger secret deal they had in the works. They had us working our tails off, getting the financials and projections for *their* sale!

This all came to a head in September of 2011—about eighteen months after our allegedly fully transparent investors had become my partners "for life"—when my assistant read a Google alert on "Pavestone Company" that said they had sold out all of their family holdings including the part that owned half of Pavestone.

In other words, they'd sold *our* company without ever discussing it!

I was shocked. They had claimed they were all about "full transparency" and were partnering with us for generations to come. There had been no mention of selling their family businesses, or Pavestone with it. They had apparently hoped that I'd just go along with the sale, feeling that I had no other choice.

Fortunately, I had an ace in the hole. We had insisted on putting a "right of first refusal" clause in our contract with the new investors. This meant that if they ever wanted to sell their half of the company, I had the option to buy it before they could accept any outside offers.

"Not so fast," I told their team.

My partner tried to deny that there was such a clause in our contract, but they were wrong. He told me not try to play lawyer, but I knew how to read a contract! And this time, there was a true angel hovering overhead.

With some difficulty, we found out that our partners had sold their half of Pavestone for about 40 percent more than they paid for it—even though they had just recently offered us 60 percent less than they paid us for our half. I could block their sale if I could come up with that amount of money to buy out their half.

Of course, I didn't have that sort of cash in hand, but lo and behold, this time, a true angel appeared. Over the years, we had kept on good terms with the folks at Quikrete in Atlanta, who had always expressed an interest in buying Pavestone, but either their offered price was too low, or the timing was bad, so those bids had not worked out.

This time, Quikrete executives acknowledged that they had missed out on two previous attempts to buy Pavestone and didn't want to lose out again. They essentially said, "What do you need so that we don't lose it this time?"

That was music to this entrepreneur's ears!

Quikrete's leadership saw Pavestone as a turnkey operation and a natural fit, a huge platform that they could, and subsequently did, build upon to add to their position as the world's largest manufacturer of packaged concrete and cement mixes to our paving stone platform. They were willing to pay more for it because we had built such a strong foundation for future growth, with great customers in

Home Depot and Walmart, and a topnotch team of engineers and plant personnel.

Thanks to the "first rights" clause and Quikrete, I was able to buy back the shares sold to the family investors with a nice profit for them and then re-sell Pavestone. I also retained ownership of several plants that Pavestone occupied, which provided future rental income.

The price was well less than the sale blocked by the FTC, but it was fair considering the company's value at that time because it had dropped considerably during the four years of the Great Recession.

I did not complain about the Quikrete deal, believe me!

A BLESSING IN DISGUISE

When the smoke cleared and my anxiety dropped a few thousand heartbeats per minute, we came out of this series of kicks to the head with our family still intact and our future financial stability still solid. Myrna and I might have had a few years shaved off our lifetimes because of the stress, but we're still here and our love and respect for each other is stronger than ever.

Our bonds also strengthened with those who stood by us and supported us through the financial and emotional challenges. We also had several friends with sharp business minds who dropped by regularly to give us tips and moral support during the battle.

Honestly, I nearly came apart at the seams during those two or three years of struggles. I've never known such distress and depression. The love of my wife and kids and a few special friends sustained me. That is why I've stressed the importance of maintaining loving and mutually supportive relationships throughout your entrepreneurial career.

If you think being an entrepreneur and owning your own business is all about the money, well, you are just wrong, and when things go sour, which they may, you will understand why I feel that way.

When your world seems to be falling apart, those relationships can help give you perspective about what is truly important. You should understand also that the entrepreneurial skills that helped you build one company don't abandon you. Legendary radio host Kidd Kraddick always ended his show by saying, "Keep looking up because that's where it all is!"

My wise wife has helped me reframe my view of this series of unfortunate events. A few months after the Quikrete sale was completed, we both reviewed the financial plans I had in place before the FTC shot down the Pavestone sale to Oldcastle.

"Do you remember what your plans were for investing the millions in profits you thought you'd make on the deal?" she asked me.

I did remember. At the time, I had three well-known and extremely successful friends, each with their own history of highly profitable investment funds. My plan was to invest large sums with each of them. I thought that I could then sit back in retirement and watch as they grew our values.

It was a sweet dream.

But here is the startling truth.

All three of those friends' investments funds were hit hard by the recession. Two of their funds dropped to zero. If I had taken the profits from the Pavestone sale and invested with them, I likely would have lost most of it, if not all of it!

How many times in your life have you seen a failure or disappointment that seemed bad at first actually lead to good or even great outcomes? This is a perfect example of that happening.

Sometimes you have to "thank God for unanswered prayers," or maybe it was my angels?

We could have lost everything because of bad investments, but instead, as things worked out, we made enough on the eventual

Pavestone sale to begin rebuilding our financial holdings during the strong and enduring recovery that followed the recession.

LESSONS LEARNED

The 2008 to 2011 stretch proved to be very humbling and scary, but I will say that we learned a lot. I certainly will never secure business loans with personal guarantees ever again.

In telling you this painful story, my hope is that you will prepare yourself for the inevitable challenges that occur in every entrepreneur's career. Our experience makes it clear that failure is part of most every success story. You would be wise to prepare to fail, but you must also remember that even in what seem like the worst of times, better days will come.

If someone had told me at the darkest hour that I should view the Pavestone turmoil as a learning experience, I probably would have laughed in their face. So, I get it. You may not be able to shift perspective that quickly or that easily, but just know that even a severe failure is not fatal, to you or your career.

My friend and fellow Canada native Brian Derksen, retired co-chairman of Deloitte, said that staying positive and empathetic toward others in such difficult times can be a lifesaver.

"Bob is one of the most positive people I know. He rarely talks in negative terms about anything or anyone, even when he endured tough times in his business. He had people disappoint him, but he moved on. He got over it and didn't dwell on it while continuing to spread his optimistic view of the world and people."

I struggled at times during our most challenging days. Friends and family, my angels, were there for me, which made the difference. That is why I stress the importance of relationships so much in my discussions with aspiring entrepreneurs.

While we were putting this book together, we came across this letter that our son Kirby wrote to me at the height of the Pavestone crisis. His words still bring me to tears, more than a decade later, and they serve as an example of the importance of family in our lives.

Dad,

Just wanted to write a quick note to tell you that it was nice to catch up yesterday and hit some golf balls. But even more so, it was great to see your new energy for Pavestone when we went by the office!

I understand the mental drain that it must have been through this past year with everything, but you are one of the greatest business leaders in the country, and it was fun to see you as motivated about the company as I have seen you in a couple years.

We are extremely proud of what you have done to create what Pavestone is as a company today, and remember that God has a plan and everything happens for a reason.

Let's get through these trying times, and while I would like to see you less stressed at times, and working a bit less, who knows where this company can be in 3-5 years from now! Might be worth looking at a couple more key executives to take some work and stress off your back, but stay positive and be proud of the amazing company you have built since I was 2 years old.

I am very proud and honored to watch you as not only my Dad, but as the best business mentor I could ever have, and I know you will make all the right decisions with the great company you have built.

If I can help in any way to add value, I would be happy to, whether it is connecting people or being at certain meetings. Also, I wanted to tell you how much I appreciate the support you have given me over the last year with everything, from business, lawsuits, relation-

ships, etc. 2008 was a beating in many ways for all of us! Let's go have a great 2009!!!!

You are the Man Dad! And Mom, you are the Woman!

Love you both very much!

Sincerely,
Kirby

When I read that letter today, I can't help but be proud of our son for the empathy and support he had for me even as he was going through his own struggles. The success Myrna and I have had in business, despite our struggles, is nothing compared to the accomplishment of raising such fine young men and women. They are all entrepreneurs in their own rights, but even better, they are compassionate, warm, and caring human beings.

THE POWER OF FORGIVENESS IN BUSINESS

Myrna and I always tell the kids that another tool in the GOI tool kit is forgiveness, which is one of the best gifts you can give yourself, as well as those you love and care about.

You may wonder how forgiveness applies in the business world, but believe me, I've found many applications over the years as an entrepreneur. People will disappoint you, whether they are employees, or suppliers, or customers, or competitors, but you can't stay mad at them forever. That does you more harm than it does them.

Anger and resentment will eat away at you and turn you into a vengeful and bitter person. You have to get over it and one of the simplest ways to do that is to simply say, "I forgive what you did. I may not forget it, but for my own sake and to preserve my happiness, I do forgive you."

You may even want to mentally picture yourself releasing the anger from inside you. Take a deep breath, and then you never have to be angry over that person again. If you can no longer trust the individual, that's fine. Don't do business with that person anymore. But don't let anger and bitterness drag you down. Your family and friends and best employees deserve better.

I've learned to walk away from anyone who proves untrustworthy. I was once preparing to do business with a guy who bragged that he'd sued over business deals several times. That should have set off alarms (as my wife often reminds me), but I didn't walk away. I entered into a project with him to open a new market for Pavestone, but both of us lost money on the deal and, sure enough, he filed a lawsuit over it.

Don't make that mistake. Some people thrive on conflict and play deceitful games. You can't fix these people or assume they would never lie to you. Steer clear of anyone who has a history of being dishonest. Trust is essential.

If you do get burned, don't let it consume you. I can tell you from experience that when you forgive those who did you wrong, surprising things can happen. Sometimes you can even become friends and continue to do business together.

Hate and other negative feelings can destroy you if held onto. Staying positive works for the best. Sometimes what you want for your business conflicts with what someone else wants. That happens. You can have legitimate disagreements or differences of opinion with people who are just looking out for their own interests, in the same way you look out for yours.

When I have a conflict with someone, I try to understand it from their perspective and figure out a win-win. That's not always possible, but it's a good goal to have. Looking for solutions that benefit both sides also creates a healthier working environment and can lead to better things down the road.

In the early years of Pavestone, we focused mostly on commercial clients like landscape companies and builders rather than retail distributors in the do-it-yourself market. We struggled to get market share in the decorative paving market with our patented products.

We were really upset, then, when another guy in our Dallas market bought manufacturing equipment similar to ours and began making products that we had patented. I was furious and I worked up a big ball of resentment for this guy.

Our lawyers fired off a cease-and-desist letter threatening to shut him down and clean out his bank account if he continued to violate our patent rights. I thought we were in for an extended fight, but he quickly backed off and stopped making those products.

As it turned out, he was an immigrant from the Middle East and unfamiliar with patent laws in the United States. He shifted into land development and became very successful doing big projects.

I ran into him a few years after we'd threatened to sue each other. When I introduced myself, he laughed and said, "Oh you are the guy who taught me about patent law!"

Now after almost forty years, we still meet often. Each time, we begin our conversations with several minutes of teasing and laughter as we joke about what we taught each other. He has recently moved into a great home down the street from mine and we both like to think we helped each other get educated.

All was forgiven, and that's the way it should be. Life is just too short to carry around negative feelings. Be slow to anger and quick to forgive and you'll enjoy your time on this planet much more. And the people around you will enjoy being with you much more, too!

DON'T BE AFRAID TO LEAN ON FRIENDS
IN HARD TIMES

I know many entrepreneurs who've battled depression, grief, and shame when they've lost businesses, even when it was no fault of their own. I've had rough times, too. My angels came forward in those times. These family members and wise and generous friends offered their help. I humbly welcomed their offers, and benefitted greatly from their advice.

I take pride in my business success, so it wasn't easy to admit when we fell on hard times, but I'm grateful that I did. We all have our ups and downs in business; there is no shame in accepting help when you need it—as long as you are willing to be there for them when they have their own challenges.

I have two great experienced friends (among many others), one a highly regarded international lawyer, and the other a veteran Fortune 500 CEO. They both worked with me for months consulting and brainstorming during the struggling Pavestone months. Thanks to these dear friends who stood by my side: Jeff Rich and Paul Stewart.

If you are struggling or feel stuck, for God's sake, ask for help. I certainly leaned on family and friends, not to mention a lot of prayer and professional help. Talk to your circle of advisors, formal or otherwise.

This is the time to take out a deposit from relationships that you've invested in over the years. And if you can't find relief close at home, by all means, go to a professional therapist. There is no shame in that. And you may find salvation in the guidance they are trained to provide based on proven methods.

And who knows, maybe one day you can pay it forward and help others through hard times. Or you can help each other through even harder times.

THE ULTIMATE CRISIS

The Covid-19 pandemic hit while I was writing this book and it proved to be an unprecedented economic tsunami with a global impact. Our prosperous nation was brought to its knees. All businesses were impacted in one way or another.

Waking up to realize an economy that was once so lucrative has crashed overnight is mind boggling. Even if you think you have all the answers for running a successful business, a crisis like this can present formidable challenges.

Even the best and most resilient business, including sports franchises, hotels, restaurants, retail malls, travel, and entertainment were shut down. Some survived. Many others did not. The airlines were brought to their knees. The stock market was roiled. Cruise lines cancelled their voyages. Car rental companies faced bankruptcy.

This is where your philosophy of leverage really can make a difference. Some of our friends leveraged their business to the max to keep growing or investing in other opportunities. But that proved to be a dangerous approach when the entire global economy is severely impacted by a calamitous event.

I have written about the danger of taking on loans with your personal guarantees, and this was one of those occasions when that can destroy an entrepreneur. Even if you want to pay off your loans and make every effort to do so, the banks and lending institutions will want it done faster than you can probably manage.

That is why you always want to work with very established and well-funded businesses with good reputations. And it served as a reminder that entrepreneurs should not take risks unless they have the resources to survive in extremely difficult times. Even those who think they have a strong financial foundation can risk losing everything when sales are down 50 to 90 percent and they can't cover rent.

During the time of this horrific virus, entrepreneurs and business owners everywhere scrambled to deal with the devastating impact of shutdowns and loss of business, forced layoffs and termination, the breakdown of the supply chain, and the crippling fear of what might come next. This was a unique event. No one knew for sure when it would end, and what the future held.

What I took from this and from other experiences is that you have to be very careful how you leverage your business because you never know when something unexpected and unanticipated can bring tough times.

Who would ever guess that sports teams would face shutdowns that ended their seasons and locked out fans? Our son Kirby misses his sport franchises, but in retrospect, we are glad that he had sold his teams prior to the pandemic. The losses would have been astronomical for him.

Even small lucrative businesses were forced to close their doors. One businesswoman was actually jailed for a short term in Dallas as she refused to close her hair salon to adhere to the rules.

Now this is not to say that some businesses can't survive without smart management and a little luck. As the economy was grinding to a halt, our son-in-law Troy and his business partner started questioning whether they really should have purchased a bankrupt company that packaged cleaning products and other consumer goods.

Troy had left a very good job as a vice president of sales for this entrepreneurial venture. Once the pandemic started, he and his partner were worried they wouldn't be able to cover expenses and the payroll. One day, early in the pandemic, Troy was feeling low as he walked through their plant and surveyed the shutdown machinery. Then, his eyes fell upon an old container that said, "Coronavirus disinfectant."

I wouldn't have blamed Troy if he'd thought it was a mirage, considering that he'd never heard the term "Coronavirus" until the Covid-19 crisis descended. But upon investigating, he discovered that the previous owners of the company had developed and won approval for a disinfectant and hand sanitizer formula many years earlier in response to the 2003 SARS outbreak, which was a close cousin of Covid-19, and subsequent flu outbreaks. This product had previously had very small sales, mostly to veterinary clinics.

What happened next is the stuff of movies. Troy and his partner scrambled to gear up production of the sanitizer, which was one of the most sought-after materials during the pandemic. Once word got out that their company was once again making their product, the big box stores were clamoring for exclusive rights to carry it and even offering to finance new machinery to produce it.

Virtually overnight, Troy's "rescue" business went from potential bankruptcy to nice seven-digit monthly sales.

This story captures both the terror and the joy of being an entrepreneur and owning your own business. You never know what awaits you around the corner! But you need to be on the corner and ready for any and every opportunity that comes your way.

With all of that said, once the Covid vaccines were developed and millions of people received the shots, the demand for hand sanitizers plummeted. Troy's company took a hit and he has struggled to raise capital and grow this business in the last quarter of 2021.

Boom or bust, most businesses are cyclical, and entrepreneurs have to be alert for changing markets. Hard times will come. Challenges will arise. But if you are knocked off your feet, do yourself and your loved ones a favor. Get back up and Get Over It! G.O.I!

LEARNING FROM FAILURE AND MOVING ON

As trite as that may sound, there is power in learning from your mistakes and moving on without looking back. Some of my closest friends have had setbacks that put them hundreds of millions and even a billion dollars in the hole, and they fought their way back to incredible wealth.

My friend Jim, the former CEO of 7-Eleven and later, Blockbuster, has weathered the ups and downs of business at a high level. He offered his perspective:

> *"Bob and I are members of the Horatio Alger Organization, as are many of our friends. This organization recognizes those who have attained success after experiencing serious adversity in their lives, whether poverty, health issues, or other challenges," Jim says. "Like me, Bob came from humble beginnings and built successful businesses. He has faced challenges that could have brought him to the edge of bankruptcy along the way, but others can learn from the way he handled adversity with grace and a sense of calm. He remained strong and persevered and even reached out to help others while his own situation was touch and go. Most people never would have known what he was going through at the time."*

That's what entrepreneurs do! We fail. We get over it. Then we apply what we've learned, along with our persistence and doggedness, to keep doing what we love.

GALLERY

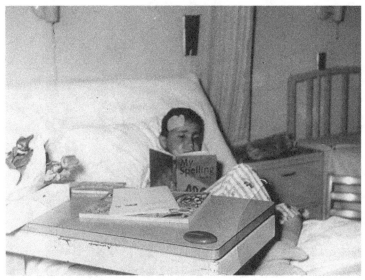

Bob hospitalized after Great Dane attack

Graduation

Schlegel wedding, 1972

Pavestone

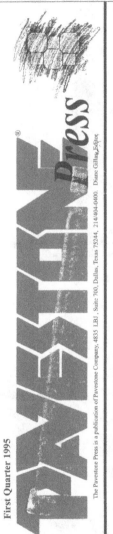

First Quarter 1995

The Pavestone Press is a publication of Pavestone Company, 4835 LBJ, Suite 700, Dallas, Texas 75244, 214-404-0400. Diane Gillay, Editor

PAVESTONE NAMED SUPPLIER OF THE YEAR

Pavestone kicked off the year with honors by capturing Payless Cashways' 1994 Building Supplier of the Year Award. Of the literally hundreds of vendors doing business with Payless Cashways, only five are selected for recognition each year. And, Pavestone is the only concrete company in Payless Cashways' history to win the coveted Supplier of the Year Award!

In presenting the award to Pavestone at a Suppliers Dinner in Kansas City, Ron Long, Vice President of Building Products for Payless Cashways, stated, "In two short years, they have taken the terms *service and quality* to the next level. Their philosophy is quite simple: to manufacture high-quality products, combined with an aggressive marketing plan, adding to it superior service, and you get a Positive Customer Experience . . . It must have been successful because the growth in purchases was an increase of better than 170% in 1994."

Long continued, "The beauty of these products for Payless is that they are used in residential as well as commercial applications and for both segments of our customer base. This winning supplier has in-

vested in people, technology, displays and us. Needless to say, we will be increasing our business with this supplier in 1995 to service our stores in 19 states, with a planned increase in purchases of 200%!"

Pavestone and Payless Cashways enjoyed their first full year of business together in 1992, with the introduction of paving products to only their Texas stores. Today Pavestone's products can be found in some 142 Payless Cashways stores in an ever-increasing number of states.

"Pavestone has exceptional quality and service, which has propelled them to the top of the industry and in the eyes of Payless Cashways," says Don James, Director of Plywood and Lumber for Payless. "The growth of our two companies together for the years to come will redefine the way these products are promoted and perceived in the United States."

Pictured at the Suppliers Dinner in Kansas City are (top row left to right) Allen Peters, Payless Cashways; Don James, Payless Cashways; Bret Scullion, Pavestone; David Stanley, Payless Cashways; Bobby Staten, Pavestone; Susan Stanton, Payless Cashways; Ron Butler, Payless Cashways; Ron Long, Payless Cashways; Larry Stonum, Payless Cashways; (bottom row left to right) George Gilbert, Pavestone; Cheri Streeter, Pavestone; Shelley Jackson, Payless Cashways; Dave Nichols, Payless Cashways; Barbara Brooks, Payless Cashways; and Dave Streeter, Pavestone.

Pavestone Press

"Perseverance Paves Way to Profits"—*Dallas Morning News*, March 20, 1994
(© 1994 The Dallas Morning News, Inc.)

Schlegel kids
(Photo by John Derryberry)

"Entrepreneur of the
Year"—*Dallas Morning
News*, June 21, 1998

Couple plants business roots

DAWN WALTON
The Globe and Mail

EDUCATION

The Schlegels, who left Kitchener-Waterloo for Texas to expand their health care venture, are donating $2-million so Canadians can learn a thing or two about entrepreneurship.

Twenty years ago, Robert and Myrna Schlegel couldn't see a way to expand their health care business in Canada. So they did what many entrepreneurs do — they uprooted to Texas.

"There's a lot of things we liked about the atmosphere there," Mrs. Schlegel recalls. "A lot of things we could do there, we couldn't do in Canada."

The free-enterprise climate has suited the Schlegels. They've built and sold a thriving nursing home chain in the Lone Star state. Now, they're riding a fast-growth business in paving stones.

But they haven't forgotten Canada. Last week, the couple announced they were giving $2-million to the university Mr. Schlegel attended and where the high school sweethearts were married — Wilfrid Laurier in Waterloo, Ont.

The funds will help build a $4-million centre for the study of entrepreneurship and technology at the university. Construction could start in 18 months.

Mr. Schlegel says there's an impression that Canadians are a little behind Americans in terms of entrepreneurial attitude. The United States, he says, leans more toward the private sector and free enterprise. "Maybe this will give Canada a little bit of a boost."

Supporting entrepreneurship is a natural for Mr. Schlegel, 48, a chartered accountant, and Mrs. Schlegel, 46, a registered nurse. They tested their operational savvy providing care to the elderly at two retirement nursing homes in southwestern Ontario during the 1970s. The business flourished, but they found there were limits.

Ultimately, Canada's public medical system drove them and their retirement-home concept south. In Texas, "we were able to be very creative in things we were doing," Mrs. Schlegel says.

By creative, she means they could charge clients more for a variety of services. Private-pay health care proved lucrative for the couple, who both come from the Mennonite community in the Kitchener-Waterloo region. They retain close ties to the community despite the distance and years that have passed.

Mr. Schlegel graduated in 1972 with a degree in economics from Wilfrid Laurier, then called Waterloo Lutheran University. The same year, he married Myrna Horst at the university's Keffer Memorial Chapel.

The two say they hope to pass on what they've learned to would-be entrepreneurs studying at the proposed Schlegel Centre for Entrepreneurial Studies. Both espouse the three "E" formula for success: Education, entrepreneurship and emotion.

"We feel Ontario will grow more and more and benefit more and more if we teach [entrepreneurship] to younger people coming along," Mrs. Schlegel says.

Geoff Malleck, a professor who teaches new venture creation at Wilfrid Laurier, says entrepreneurship departments are becoming fashionable in post-secondary institutions. "It's the flavour of the year," he says, adding that these centres will encourage more creative thinking.

But Mr. Malleck cautions that entrepreneurship is a difficult thing to teach. "It's more of a philosophy."

One Schlegel venture, Peo-

THE SCHLEGELS

Robert, 48. Chartered accountant with bachelor's degree in economics from Waterloo Lutheran, now Wilfrid Laurier University. Founded the Kitchener, Ont., accounting firm Schlegel Moore and Robertson in 1975. Co-founded Dallas-based Pavestone in 1980, president of the Ontario Nursing Home Association in 1984.

Myrna, 46. Registered nurse, graduated from Toronto General Hospital, later studied health care administration at Southern Meth-

odist University in Dallas and University of Texas in Austin. President of PeopleCare Heritage Centers in Texas until Horizon Healthcare acquired the company in 1994. Chairwoman of Schlegel Horizon Foundation, a Dallas-based philanthropic organization.

Family home is in Dallas. Four children: Kim, 22, Kirby, 20, Kari, 14, and Krystal, 9. Mrs. Schlegel's parents live in Waterloo, Ont., and Mr. Schlegel's mother lives in Tavistock, Ont.

pleCare Heritage Centers Inc., started as one small retirement centre and expanded over the years into a 2,200-bed group of 13 facilities scattered around Texas. The company gained a reputation for innovative, high-quality care.

Meanwhile, Mr. Schlegel spotted another business opportunity. A Texas real estate and construction boom in 1980 created vast possibilities in landscaping and design. Interlocking stones were extremely popular in Canada at the time, but the concrete products were not being manufactured in the U.S. Southwest.

So Mr. Schlegel and a partner set up Pavestone Co. in Dallas to begin producing the stylish stones. It was a hard sell at first, but perseverance turned to success. Seven years later, the company had three plants and 70 employees.

But the 1987 Texas oil crisis and real estate collapse slashed customer flow to the fledgling com-

pany. Pavestone struggled under a mound of debts that almost forced the company into bankruptcy.

Mr. Schlegel jokes that if he had any sense, he would have given up on the company when his partner left. Instead, he called in a small business consultant and persuaded big box retailers, such as Home Depot Inc., to stock Pavestone products for driveways, walkways and retaining walls.

Ultimately, they managed to turn the company into what Mr. Schlegel says is the largest producer of concrete landscaping products in the United States, with 10 factories and distribution to 30 states.

Sales at Pavestone reached $50-million (U.S.) in 1997 and are projected to reach $80-million this year, Mr. Schlegel hopes to hit $200-million by 2000.

The astounding growth prompted cable news network CNBC to label Pavestone a corporate "guzzle." This year, Mr. Schle-

gel was named Ernst & Young's entrepreneur of the year in the southwestern United States.

Soon after Pavestone moved back into the black, PeopleCare reached its own crossroad. The business was so successful that Horizon Healthcare Corp., a Albuquerque, N.M.-based company, had been "wining and dining" the Schlegels for years trying to entice them to sell. By 1994, both were putting in long hours at their respective businesses and the Schlegels were ready for a change.

"We also have four children who we saw growing very quickly," Mrs. Schlegel says. "We really felt like one of us needed to give and be able to spend more time with the family so [PeopleCare] was the one we decide to sell."

The deal saw Horizon pay $21-million in cash, assume debt of $35-million, as well as issue $6-million in stock to acquire the leases or titles to the 13 facilities. (Horizon has since been acquired by another U.S. firm.)

The sale helped fund the Schlegel Horizon Foundation, a philanthropic organization that supports education, health care and the arts. The foundation funded the contribution to Wilfrid Laurier — the largest single donation yet to the university.

"We started from basically scratch and I think maybe we can be an example of what folks can do with a little bit of drive and ambition," Mr. Schlegel says humbly. "I guess I'm not the world's greatest student, but somehow we managed to get through."

Robert and Myrna Schlegel say they both espouse the three "E" formula for success: Education, entrepreneurship and emotion.

"Couple Plants Business Roots"—*The Globe and Mail*, 1998

Impressions

Schlegels honored for contributions to community

Robert and Myrna Schlegel

High school sweethearts Myrna and Robert Schlegel moved to Dallas from Toronto in 1979 to start their family, their business and their lives. Entrepreneurs, philanthropists and education enthusiasts, the Schlegels quickly established deep Texas roots.

After raising a family in Dallas, the couple swears they could never leave. "Dallas has given us a wonderful life," says Myrna, "The people here are so friendly and supportive. It is fun being successful in Texas because Texans enjoy success."

The Schlegels have contributed to the Dallas community in the areas of the arts, business, education and charity. Among their contributions to education in Dallas is a recent substantial donation to Southern Methodist University. In addition, Myrna and Robert co-chaired a $6 million fundraiser for a new high school for Trinity Christian Academy. The school was completed in 1998.

Together Myrna and Robert founded the Schlegel Horizons Foundation, which promotes education, sound health care policies and arts and cultural organizations. Myrna is past president of A.W.A.R.E. and currently serves on the National Board of Alzheimer's Association. She recently co-chaired the Dallas Symphony's Opening Centennial Gala, raising a record-breaking amount for the Symphony.

Despite their love for Dallas, the Schlegels are loyal to their native Canada. Robert recently started a facility at his Ontario alma mater to promote entrepreneurship, The Schlegel Center for Entrepreneurial Studies. "We try to take back to Canada the ideas Dallas has taught us," says Robert.

While the Schlegels spend much of their time with their favorite charities, their heart is in their business. True entrepreneurs, Myrna and Robert enjoy building companies. They founded and manage The Pavestone Company, which makes concrete landscape products, including retaining walls, patio and paving stones. The Pavestone Company now employs over 800 people and is on pace to surpass the $200 million sales level.

Although many married couples keep home and office separate, Myrna and Robert have somehow managed to work together smoothly as husband and wife. "There is a great energy between us. We have different talents so we complement each other well," says Robert.

Despite their many activities, Myrna and Robert's first priority is always their family. The couple have four children, Kim - 23, Kirby - 21, Kari - 15 and Krystal - 10. The Schlegels do not believe that work should be left at the office; they often bring business to the family dinner table. "It is fun to teach your children business," says Myrna, "We let them see the good and the bad."

Kim has followed in her parents' footsteps and started her own company in Dallas: R.S.V.P. - Soiree Luxury Rentals. Kirby studies business at SMU, while Kari and Krystal are both enrolled in Trinity Christian Academy.

The National Jewish Medical and Research Center will honor Myrna and Robert Schlegel for their copious contributions to Dallas with a dinner on May 11, 2000. "The Schlegels have given so much to Dallas; we want to show them how grateful the community is," says Karla Stover, Executive Director of the National Jewish Medical and Research Center.

The dinner will be at the Wyndham Anatole Hotel and feature music by legendary Burt Bacharach, Scott Murray as master of ceremonies, and Kelly and Norman Green as chairpersons. Honorary chairmen are Paul Nussbaum, Burton Tansky and Allan Zidell. Reservations for the evening may be made by calling the office of the National Jewish Medical and Research Center at 214-559-3060.

OCTOBER · 2002

Philanthropy
IN TEXAS

Bob &
Myrna
Schlegel
The
American
Dream

Profiles
Margot & Bill
Winspear

Eugene H. Vaughan

Linda Pitts Custard

Laura & Jack
Richmond

**Philanthropy
of the West**

Bob & Myrna Schlegel

Philanthropy in Texas, October 2002

7.7.02

Style

How to Succeed in Texas by Really, Really Trying...

Some tips, y'all. By David Feld

Texas in the late 70's and early 80's was one big, baroque barbecue. Oil was $30 a barrel, real estate was booming and the savings and loans were riding high. I was in my 20's then, and all I really remember is an endless blur of parties, Champagne, lamé and really big hair. I went through three tuxedos and 15 pairs of evening pumps. Then it was over. In 1986 oil prices plummeted, the banks collapsed and the savings-and-loan scandal finished off the romp. When some formerly rich friends of mine had a "we are poor" party, I knew it was time to return to New York.

But now I'm back, and Texas is hotter than ever. I'm not talking about the weather — which as I write is pushing 90 degrees at 8 in the morning — I'm talking about the international social scene. With Vogue's Anna Wintour dating a Texan (he lives out in the middle of nowhere on a ranch in Marfa) and yet another Bush in the White House, New York and European socialites are making pilgrimages to the Lone Star State like horses back to the barn. As many of us learned during the wretched excess of the 80's, it's not that hard to make it big in Texas society. But here's a bit of advice:

• You never ask a Texan how big his ranch is. (That's like asking the size of his bank balance, or worse.)

• You tell everyone that you sold Enron at $90 and that *Continued on Page 42*

On the junior circuit, Kim Schlegel, center, in a BCBG Max Azria silk chiffon dress, $904. At BCBG Max Azria boutiques. Tommy Hilfiger's wool pinstripe suit, $425, and tie. For information call (888) 866-6948. Robert Talbott cotton shirt, $135, and pocket square. At Robert Talbott boutiques. Halston jersey gown, $1,300. At Saks Fifth Avenue. All jewelry: William Noble.

35

Schlegel Center for Entrepreneurship Grand Opening, 2003

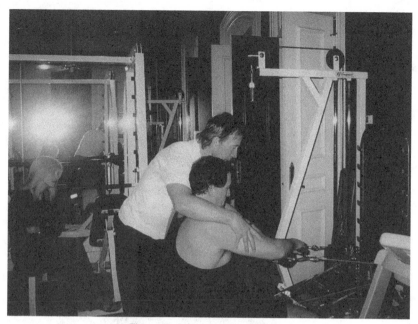

Fitness Training with Chuck Norris

Dallas Morning News, January 4, 2004

Rainers, November 30, 2006 (© 2006 McClatchy. All rights reserved. Used under license.)

Schlegel family and Tornado hockey team, 2006

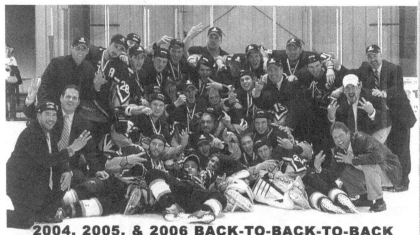

2004, 2005, & 2006 BACK-TO-BACK-TO-BACK
NAHL ROBERTSON CUP NATIONAL CHAMPIONS

NAHL Back to Back Champions, 2006

Bob and Kirby Hockey
Team Travelers

Dallas Morning News, April 11, 2007

Highs and Lows

COVERING THE DALLAS-FORT WORTH METROPLEX

Dallas Business Journal

FTC suit puts kibosh on Pavestone merger

Grapevine concrete landscape company weighs options after $540 million proposed buyout gets negative review

BY KATHERINE CROMER BROCK | STAFF WRITER

Grapevine-based Pavestone Co. LP has dropped plans to merge with an Ireland-based competitor after the Federal Trade Commission filed a lawsuit in an attempt to block the $540 million union.

In court documents, the FTC cited concerns about the new company creating what it considered to be an unfair advantage — but Pavestone's outraged chief executive doesn't see it that way.

"We thought it could have been good for

Texas and good for the whole country," said Pavestone founder and CEO Bob Schlegel. "It's really disappointing."

Schlegel said business will continue as usual at the company which produces segmented concrete for landscaping, and he will now seek private investors to bolster

PAVESTONE, P18

STAYING SOLID: CEO Bob Schlegel is on site at Pavestone's Grapevine plant, one of 16 nationwide.

Dallas Business Journal (© Dallas Business Journal, 2/6/2009.
All rights reserved. Reprinted with permission.)

Justice Clarence Thomas presents Horatio Alger Award

Bob receives the Horatio Alger Award, 2008

Moonwalker Buzz Aldrin—Horatio Alger member

D CEO "Schlegel Family Values" (Photo by Dan Sellers, 2009)

With former Prime Minister of Canada, Brian Mulroney—also a Horatio Alger member

Myrna, my angel

Bob and Myrna (Photo by Jin Kim Studio)

Bob riding on the Silverwood Master Planned Community Land
in the Mojave River Valley, Hesperia, California

Discussing KPIs at Bedrock Logistics

Examining our Solarstone prototype

Bob's toast at his last daughter, Krystal's wedding
(Photo by John Cain)

My family is still growing
(Photo by John Cain)

Chapter Eight

BUSINESS WITH A PURPOSE

I celebrated my seventieth birthday while writing this book, and I have no intention of slowing down my entrepreneurial career. In fact, I have three or four ventures in the works that are aligned with my new passion for creating companies and projects that do well while also doing good in our world.

One of them has the potential to revolutionize the way we bring power to our homes and businesses. Another serves an emerging need in public safety and law enforcement, and the third will help address parts of our nation's chronic affordable housing shortage. And a fourth is an investment I made a few years ago with a couple Canadian friends to take over an abandoned Northern Ontario lumber mill.

The lumber industry is directly affected by swings in lumber commodity prices, which in 2020 and 2021 went up almost 500 percent and of course settled back down in short order. It was one of those rare opportunities to quickly pay off our debt and completely de-leverage the company to save our "cash cow."

This unexpected development also helped restore jobs at the mill that were lost during a downturn years earlier. A win-win. This series of fortunate events exhibits my advice about trying to be on the corner when the bus of opportunity stops.

DOING WELL WHILE DOING GOOD

I am looking for similar projects in this rapidly growing field, which I call "social impact entrepreneurship," for lack of a better term. The general idea is to address a societal need with creative methods that are sustainable and profitable, so they generate income and jobs while benefitting our communities and our world.

Social entrepreneurship takes business practices such as goal setting, results measurements, financial sustainability, and scaled systems, and uses them to solve challenges in our world including social needs and sustainability issues.

Some have described this type of win-win enterprise as impact investing or a "triple-bottom line" business because the goal is to serve the business owners with a fair return on capital, but also to serve the needs of other people and the overall planet.

Think of it as pursuing a profit with a purpose. We started this approach early on in our healthcare business with our life-enrichment programs for our residents and at Pavestone Company with our goal to assist customers and "improve your landscape." When we think back, we were always working with a purpose to improve the lives of our clients.

Social impact entrepreneurship is spreading around the world, and it encompasses a wide range of fields and approaches. Our friend Trisha Wilson, the renowned grand hotel interior designer, is one example I know. In her forty-year career designing interiors for high-end resorts, casinos, tourist attractions, and residences around the world, she always made it a point to employ local crafts people and vendors whenever possible to benefit local economies.

If the locals needed additional or specialized training, she brought in experts, including Disney Imagineers, to teach them what they needed to know to work on her projects. Trisha told me she and her team often spent days searching for artists and craftspeople they had heard about in their projects across Asia, Europe, and Africa.

She once saw a carving in a local market in South Africa that she thought would work in one of her projects, so she tracked down the artist by going to a farm where he worked as the night watchman. "Hopefully, what we paid him helped that artist provide for his family for many years," she said.

In her Dallas headquarters and at their eleven other offices around the globe, which employed as many as 700 people, Trisha instituted policies that encouraged employees to use their time and talents to benefit their communities.

For example, at a high school in a depressed area of Dallas, where sixteen languages were spoken due to the diverse immigrant population, her employees volunteered as tutors, painters, and fundraisers for school projects.

In my research, I've found other practitioners of social impact entrepreneurism with a wide range of companies that:

- Create healthy and tasty raw and organic foods to encourage better diets

- Promote eco-adventure travel meant to connect tourists with native cultures in ways that benefit both

- Design solutions for pressing social problems in foster care, criminal justice, and healthcare

- Dig wells in parts of the world with severe water scarcity

- Preserve and encourage artisan craftmanship around the world

- Use profits to fund clean water projects in needy areas

- Make watches for the blind

- Create designer bags from recycled plastic from the ocean and landfills

- Provide tractors and other machinery to poor farmers in Africa
- Produce organic hand soap and donates a bar to Haitian orphanages for every one sold.

Another great example of using the tools you have to help others in need is the Dallas Cowboys, who raise millions of dollars for the Salvation Army every year. Similarly, Northpark Mall, which has twenty-six-million people come through their doors, fills their hallways with non-profit signage to help community organizations in need.

Even if the main focus of your business is not currently about giving back or social entrepreneurship, you can still find ways to make an impact on your community by using the tools that you already have—and that makes all of your hard work a lot more fulfilling.

You get the idea. There is a rapidly growing movement to create companies, both for-profit and non-profit, that contribute to a greater good.

FINDING A NEED AND FILLING IT

Like many social impact entrepreneurs, they see a need and then put together a self-sustaining for-profit business to serve it. My partner, Joe Byles, in an exciting new venture has done much the same thing in his career. Joe is an aeronautical engineer, inventor, and entrepreneur who uses his considerable brainpower to light up the world, literally.

He holds more than twenty patents in the U.S. and abroad, many of them in the solar energy field, but he began his career in an entirely different arena. While still in his early twenties, he made an interesting decision. He was just out of college and working for a major aeronautics corporation when he developed an avionics system for military fighter aircraft that won design awards and proved to be a boon to the industry.

Strangely enough, it was a compliment from a U.S. Air Force general at an awards ceremony that convinced Joe to change the course of his career. The general told him: "You made the information system for our guided bombs much more accurate."

He accepted the award and the gratitude, but he was troubled at the thought of using his gifts to create more efficient tools of destruction. "I had an existential moment," he said. "I was twenty-two, and I didn't want to be a cog in a company with thousands of other engineers and I didn't want to help kill people with bombs."

Instead, he decided to focus on creating products and companies engaged in more benevolent fields like sustainable "green" products, solar power, water conservation, and vegetative roofs.

Over the decades that followed, he developed a number of innovative products, including a rooftop solar panel system that doesn't have to be screwed into the roof. His creations are sold at Home Depot and other major retailers.

Joe heard about my entrepreneurial businesses from mutual friends at Home Depot, and he began calling me with an idea for a new product in 2018. I put him off a couple of times, just because I was involved with other projects, but when we finally sat down for a meeting, I was glad we did.

On that first day, Joe came into my office carrying a couple patio paving stones—items I was very familiar with, of course. I thought, *This guy is trying to sell concrete pavers to* me?

But as I discovered, Joe's paving stones were unlike any I'd ever seen since starting my Pavestone company forty years ago. His pavers had a much more significant feature. Our meeting was supposed to last an hour, but it went on for four or five. Then I had him get together with a few of my manufacturing and business associates the next day.

You might say Joe got my attention. In a nutshell, Joe's concept has the potential to revolutionize not just the solar power industry, but the entire world of power generation. Basically, it's a solar panel embedded in a concrete patio stone that can serve as patios, sidewalks, and pool decks.

LIGHTING UP

We see this as a business with the potential for enormous societal benefits. Before I go deeper into Joe's concept, I want to give you a brief history of the power industry that lights up your homes and offices.

In the early days of electricity, there were no giant power companies or power plants like PG&E, Duke, or Canada's Ontario Hydro. The first water-powered generators worked by spinning magnets through coils similar to those at Niagara Falls, which still produce hydroelectric power today.

Only rich people with relatively small residences could afford to have those generators, but they had full control over the power to their homes. There were some early mom-and-pop power companies with generators that supplied electricity to a few wealthy homeowners or businesses, but it took generations to develop the power grid that we use today.

Over time, inventors came up with larger generating systems in centralized plants that could be distributed through a much more elaborate and extensive grid system. Thomas Edison and partners created the first big power company, Edison Electric Illuminating Company, to light up a part of Manhattan in 1882.

By 1925, still only half of the homes in the United States had electric power. The big power companies and their plants have helped make electricity affordable for most people, rather than just the wealthiest. But that meant customers were at the mercy of those dominant power companies.

What if someone came along who could put control over your home's electricity back in your hands? What if we all had a financially feasible way to generate enough power for our homes and businesses?

The value of a product that could put power back in the control of each consumer became even more clear to me in November 2019, when I saw on the local news that there were 450,000 people in Northern California without power to their homes.

Their power company, Pacific Gas & Electric, preemptively shut off their electricity due to the potential threat for fires from sparking and downed powerlines because of high winds in that region.

The number of people affected by the power shutoff was only half of what it had been a few weeks earlier, in October 2019. The PG&E shutdowns were highly controversial because they were involuntary for customers, who, quite rightly, were outraged.

A power company is supposed to provide electricity to its customers who pay for that service. PG&E was facing bankruptcy. While watching the news coverage of this controversy, I kept thinking, "We have the potential answer to this critical societal problem, and we are working on bringing it to reality right now."

That would be a boon to not just Californians, but to all of society, right?

Well, as I write this, my new business partner and I are busy putting together a product and a business plan that will offer a line of affordable solar power generating patio stone-type products. The business is called SolarStone. These concrete pavers with embedded solar energy panels provide all the power necessary to light up a home, and run all of your appliances, including your air-conditioning system.

This product isn't just a backup for when your power fails; it can generate power whenever the sun is shining, and then the power can be stored on battery packs for use twenty-four-seven. All year. Every year.

Joe deserves full credit for coming up with this concept. Along with holding a bachelor's degree from the University of Texas-Austin in aerospace, aeronautical, and astronautical engineering, and all those patents, he is also a master gardener.

So, he's the science and engineering wizard with a green thumb. I'm the numbers guy with many years of experience manufacturing and distributing patio stones and landscaping products.

As partners in this new company, we have complementary skill-sets, but we also have a few things in common. We each have owned successful companies. We've each had some business failures and made mistakes over the course of our careers. And hopefully, we've both learned from them, and are better (or certainly more experienced) as a result.

DOING BUSINESS AND DOING GOOD

What really brought us together as partners in this new and exciting venture is our shared desire to make a positive difference in this world, while also creating jobs through a for-profit, sustainable business.

As I write this, we are working on refining our first product for SolarStone and securing Department of Energy (DOE) approvals. We've put together some members of my old band, so to speak, from my Pavestone Company, to help us bring his creation into a mass-market reality.

In a nutshell, our goal is to manufacture paving stones with built-in solar power cells that will generate electricity on their surface (literally). They will look like standard concrete patio slabs used for pool decks, sidewalks, and patios, but solar energy will be able to penetrate the surface and reach the solar panel embedded in it, generating similar electricity as roof-mounted solar panels!

Our products won't be as durable as regular pavers, but they can handle pedestrian traffic when used to build a patio. You wouldn't want to permanently cover these solar power pavers with patio furniture or your BBQ grill for extended periods because they need exposure to sunlight to do their job.

A twenty-four-foot square patio with SolarStone pavers would generate five thousand watts of energy that can be used for your home or office or be stored for later use in a battery pack we can also make available. It will be easier to install and maintain with similar costs to a rooftop solar system.

This is a major leap in the energy field, and it makes sense economically and environmentally. Our system doesn't burn oil or natural gas, so it helps drive carbon out of the power grid system.

Another big benefit is the fact that our paver patios can be installed by most do-it-yourselfers. They will need a professional electrician to hook up the SolarStone system to their homes, but the engineering and installation cost will be substantially less than that for an ugly rooftop solar system.

The plan is to sell SolarStone products through the major wholesalers and big-box retail stores, in the same way we marketed Pavestone products. We are already looking at arranging for manufacturing in strategic parts of the country.

This is still a work in progress, but it is very exciting. We've even had a top official with the U.S. Department of Energy tell us that this would revolutionize the power industry.

I can't help but think what a welcome relief our SolarStone products will be for the people in California, who have had their power shut off due to the threat of forest fires. That would never happen to them again. This power source can't be blown away or burned out. Not to mention, it can supply power to rural areas of the world where there is no power grid.

We believe this could be a game changer. We believe these solar power pavers will change our world for the better in a big way. We hope SolarStone's products will be a boon to consumers and benefit our world while creating jobs and a cleaner environment. We recently received a patent on our SolarStone and we are finalizing manufacturing techniques.

BUILDING A BETTER WORLD

There is another reason I was so excited when Joe came to me with this product design. Solar power pavers also will benefit another social impact business I've spent the last several years developing in California.

There is a dramatic shortage of affordable starter homes across much of the United States, especially in California. *The Wall Street Journal* and other news outlets have reported the need for 7.5 million new homes in the U.S., including 3.4 million needed in California. This shortage has driven up demand and driven up the value of homes in that state, where the average home price is now $540,000.

The greatest need in that state is for lower-cost homes in a range affordable for young couples, first-time homebuyers, and retirees. I saw an opportunity to address that problem several years ago when I learned about a stalled Master Planned Community in development located on about ten thousand acres in Hesperia, California, in the Mojave River Valley.

This area on the edge of what Californians call the "Inland Empire" was referred to as the "High Desert" and is within commuting distance of the greater San Bernardino-Riverside Los Angeles Basin.

This ambitious residential project is one of the largest housing projects in Southern California, which began planning in 1985. The original developers were met with substantial opposition from environmentalists and residents. They were concerned about the impact of more than fifteen thousand new residences. Construction would go on for more than two decades and bring an estimated fifty thousand new residents to the area.

Lawsuits and resistance from environmental groups went on for decades. I invested in the project after seeing the opportunity to revise the master plan and collaborate with local interest groups to make the project work. What could be better than providing much-needed affordable housing in a beautiful part of California while also creating thousands of jobs?

Our team had to clear a lot of hurdles in the last nine years, but construction on the first homes in the project currently known as "Silverwood" will go on the market in 2022. The new plan features protected nature areas, as well as solar energy, water recycling, xeriscapes to reduce irrigation demands, and hundreds of miles of walkable neighborhood trails.

This project ties in well with our SolarStone enterprise because California requires every newly constructed home to have a solar system, so builders are looking for the safest, most affordable, attractive, and durable ways to do that. We think the Silverwood community will be the perfect place to put our solar-energy pavers out there in a big way.

Any enterprise I start or join these days, whether it is solar power-generating pavers or an environmentally friendly community that provides much-needed housing, is designed to contribute to a better world in some way. I am also trying to pave the way, pardon the expression, for other social impact entrepreneurs by encouraging this form of business at the Schlegel Centre for Entrepreneurship and Social Innovation, which has a LaunchPad incubator at Wilfrid Laurier University, my alma mater in Canada.

The center conducts an annual Changemaker Innovation Challenge. This is a qualifying competition for the much larger global Map the System Challenge, run by the Skoll Centre for Social Entrepreneurship at the University of Oxford in Great Britain.

The competition calls for students who are passionate about social and environmental challenges to study them in-depth and then come up with for-profit or non-profit businesses that address those issues.

In recent competitions, our students focused on issues including income inequality in the Greater Toronto area, pollution in the Yangtze River, sexual violence in varsity athletics, and poverty in Niger.

I mentioned earlier in the book that I've invested in Guard-Ex, a start-up created by current and former students at the Schlegel Centre. Let me tell you a bit more about this company's innovative roadside-screening device for law enforcement. It is less expensive, faster, and takes any question of bias out of testing for alcohol, cannabis, and drug intoxication.

Individuals metabolize drugs and alcohol differently. A driver who tests positive for cannabis with a standard breathalyzer may not be impaired. Other screening devices, including those that test for alcohol consumption, simply measure for the levels of a substance. The Guard-Ex device screens directly for impairment.

The students who came up with the idea for this great innovation had hosted a lot of parties and they were worried about people who had been drinking and smoking pot driving home. The device they came up with measures eye movement, body temperature, and heart activity that can indicate impairment.

A BUDDY IN BLUE

I invested the initial capital into this company after I ran the concept by my boyhood buddy and lifelong friend, Larry Gravill, who was in law enforcement for thirty-eight years, serving as police chief for our hometown Waterloo Regional Police Force for fifteen years.

Larry and I have been friends since we were thirteen years old and high school freshman. In fact, even today when we get together or talk on the phone we seem to revert back to our teenage years, kidding with each other and telling stories from our school days.

He and his wife Debbie were dating back then, and I was already trying to hook up with Myrna. She and Debbie were friends too, so we double dated a lot.

When Myrna and Debbie were in nursing college in Toronto, Larry and I often drove there together in my Mercury Cougar with a roaring 335 horsepower engine. We still laugh about the time he and I got into a snowball fight while we were waiting for the girls to come out to the car so we could drive them home for the weekend.

I was whipping snowballs at him and Larry tried to duck back into the car just as I nailed him in the top of the head. When he tried to dodge, his face slammed into the frame of the car door that he'd just opened.

His nose bled all the way home, which put a damper on our double date. In fact, when we returned home, we had to take poor Larry to the hospital, where they packed his nose with cotton to stop the bleeding.

I felt like a real jerk, but he forgave me. He was the king of pranks, so it wasn't the last time I made him the target of one of my own pranks. We both attended Wilfrid Laurier University in Waterloo after high school and remained close. Near the end of our second year, we were talking about future plans and Larry surprised me by saying he was considering a career in law enforcement.

He'd even looked at applying for a job with the Ontario Provincial Police (OPP) department in Waterloo's larger "sister" city of Kitchener. We talked about it a bit and he was so enthusiastic, I just blurted out, "Let's go get applications!"

"Really? You want to apply, too?"

"Sure, we can be a crime-fighting duo, like Batman and Robin."

We drove down to police headquarters that day and picked up our applications. I'll let Larry tell the story from there:

So, I diligently filled out the application and sent it in, thinking Bob and I were on our way to becoming police officers together. About six weeks. later, I got a follow-up letter from the department, inviting me to come in for an interview.

I was so excited. When I saw Bob, I said, "How are things going with your application? They asked me to come in for an interview. It would be great if we went in at the same time!"

"What application?" he replied.

Then, Bob broke out laughing. "You can go be a cop," he said. "I'm going to be an accountant. I threw my application away!"

Bob thought it was all very funny.

I was crushed. We had done so many things together, I thought it would be terrific if we could be partners on the police force. But my buddy bailed on me!

Larry went on to a great career. He was the chief in charge of a thousand officers in our regional police department, and he was also a leader and board member of national and international police organizations.

I had a few sleepless nights thinking Larry might send a SWAT team after me as revenge someday, but fortunately he forgave me.

I always encouraged him in his police career, but whenever we get together and have a drink or two, he always brings up the fact that I led him to believe I was joining him in the police department, and then abandoned him to join an accounting firm.

At Larry's retirement dinner, I had the opportunity to roast him, and I let him know, "If I had signed up with you, I'm sure one of us would have been a good deputy in chief."

Larry can take a joke, which proved to be a good thing for my mother. You see, she always reprimanded Larry and me for driving too fast when we were young, but she was known to have a heavy foot behind the wheel, herself.

One day Larry was on patrol and spied a speeding car going well over the limit. Excited about making an arrest, he gave chase all the way to my brother-in-law's home.

He was shocked when he saw my mother pop out of the driver's seat, but my mom didn't give him a chance to make an arrest.

She took one look at him and said, "Oh, it's just you, Larry! You scared me. I thought it was a real cop!"

Nice put-down, Mom!

A FRIEND IN CHIEF

I'm telling you this story because in recent years, Larry has been a terrific asset in giving a boost to the Guard-Ex business. You see, entrepreneurs can sometimes feel isolated and alone as they strive to succeed. They feel they have to focus on their business goals to the exclusion of their relationships. But I'm proof that this is not true, and our friendship has also blossomed into a business relationship with this company.

To build this start-up, we needed to get the word out to law enforcement officials that there was a new device that screens subjects for impairment from cannabis. The young entrepreneurs who developed that device and founded Guard-Ex had worked hard to get traction with local police departments. They'd made a few inroads, but they had encountered challenges getting police officials to approve trials of the device in the field.

I encouraged Larry to get involved. I said, "You know so many police chiefs from law enforcement organizations that you belonged to and lead, maybe you could help open doors for Guard-Ex."

Now, Larry was enjoying retirement and sort of had his own plans, but I knew he wouldn't turn me down, especially since he was a champion of public safety and the Guard-Ex device would be very helpful to police departments dealing with the legalization of marijuana across Canada and growing use by the public.

He has since stepped up and done a great job of making the initial pitches and getting our Guard-Ex team in the door so they can develop a market once the device is certified.

We've also had big trucking firms express interest in Guard-Ex because it also measures for driver fatigue. Companies that employ pilots and heavy-equipment operators will also be target markets.

At Pavestone, I always stressed the motto, "Safety first, then quality, then quantity," and this is a product that will improve safety on the road and workplace for everyone. I think that's a great benefit to society.

SOMETHING SMALL CAN CHANGE THE WORLD

I'm also excited that one of our Schlegel Centre student start-ups in the social impact field was a finalist in a *National Geographic* competition—a global search for innovative ways to help tackle the world's single-use plastic problem. This company is called Earth Suds, and its products were created to replace the 5.7 billion shampoo, soap, and lotion hotel shower bottles that end up in landfills each year.

These students have come up with a brand of dissolvable tablets that are transformed into shampoo, conditioner, and bodywash in the shower. Their main target market is the hotel industry, where concerns have grown about the use of plastic bottles that can't be recycled.

Earth Suds founder Marissa Vettoretti, aged twenty, who worked with chemistry students to come up with her product, said campers will also find the dissolvable tablets useful.

When I visit the Schlegel Centre, I love hanging out with the dynamic young people in our program. They have really embraced the concept of doing well by doing good in this world. Their generation is incredibly tuned into finding ways to make the world cleaner, safer, and more accepting.

They tend to teach me more than I could ever teach them because they come from such diverse backgrounds and experiences.

One of those students, Hillary Scanlon, came up with another award-winning product that I never could have dreamed of. Hillary is legally blind, and it bothered her that when she took her dorm room trash out to her student housing receptacles, she couldn't tell which were for recyclables and which were for regular garbage. I love that she didn't just shrug it off, but instead developed a product that solved her problem and benefitted the environment.

She came up with thin, rubber floor tiles of different tactile types that can be placed in front of garbage, recycling and compost receptacles so that those with vision challenges can detect the proper containers by using their canes or feet.

Hillary calls her business Sustainability Through an Inclusive Lens, and I called it a brilliant, simple, and effective solution. I love the enthusiasm these young entrepreneurs show for their businesses. They are combining social activism with entrepreneurship to make a difference in this world while chasing their dreams of running sustainable companies that create jobs for their communities and financial security for themselves and their families.

Seriously, when it comes to business, it doesn't get any better than that! I encourage entrepreneurs of all ages to look for similar opportunities.

Chapter Nine

TO WHOM MUCH IS GIVEN: PHILANTHROPY WITH A PURPOSE

"It is more difficult to give money away intelligently than to earn it in the first place."

~Andrew Carnegie

As a boy, I braved black bears and polar bears to accompany my father on his trips into "the Gateway to the Arctic" in far northern Ontario.

You see, my dad was a part time "Shantyman."

That title didn't mean he lived in a shack. He was a member of the Shantymen's Christian Association, which carried out evangelical mission work among loggers and miners in the bush camps way up on the shores of Hudson Bay.

Once a year or so, he'd drive a small 1950 Chevrolet panel truck more than 500 miles north to remote lumber camps, jails, and prisons, in rugged places like Moosonee, Moose Factory, Kapuskasing, and Cochrane.

My sister Mary, who is five years older, remembers thinking back then that I was lucky to get to go on those adventures with our father.

"It was just boys and men up there, and my dad and Bob would go up to share our faith with them—everything was centered around church and community growing up," she recalled.

My father lugged in a heavy movie projector and he'd show Bible films to the lumberjacks and prisoners, sharing our faith and offering hope and encouragement. My father was a kind and generous man. Even when he struggled with the farm in the hard times and worried about losing everything, he still paid the heating bills for our church.

My mother was also active in the community. She volunteered as a chef in children's camps and I would go along, which was always a treat.

Myrna's parents were also service oriented. Her mother's main focus was serving as a foster parent. My wife lived with more than thirty-five different foster kids over the years. Sometimes there were four or five of them in the house, along with Myrna and her four siblings, which meant a lot of sacrifices for them all.

This made for some interesting experiences and interactions. Myrna had to constantly share her toys with the children moving in and out of their home. She had some trouble with this when she was very young, especially when one foster sister latched on to Myrna's beloved toy baby buggy given to her by her father.

The foster child broke Myrna's heart by cutting up the buggy's fabric, shredding it to pieces.

"I was crying and told my mother that I hated that girl," Myrna recalled saying. "But then my mom said, 'Let her keep it for now. You have family who love you, so you have way more than she has already.'"

The message that love is the greatest gift always stayed with Myrna. We both were taught, through actions more than words, that serving and giving to others was part of our faith.

We've tried to follow that philanthropic philosophy over the years even as we raised our children and built our businesses. And we've discovered, sometimes giving to others can become as complicated and tricky as having a family and running a couple companies at once.

CHARITY WITH CLARITY

My point is that you have to put as much thought into your good deeds as you do into your businesses and parenting. Early on, especially, we made mistakes even though we had good intentions to give to worthy causes.

In sharing our missteps in philanthropy, I'm hoping you can learn from us and avoid making those same mistakes. You see, we gave generously for years without any kind of plan. We'd just contribute time or money to charities or causes or organizations when they came to us or somehow got our attention.

When we were building our businesses from the ground up, we didn't consider ourselves wealthy because we weren't. Any money that we made, we put back into our companies, hiring more people and adding more facilities. In those early days, most of our donations and efforts went to local groups, our church and our kids' schools and teams.

It wasn't until we sold our Heritage Nursing and Retirement Centers that it dawned on us that we needed a philanthropy strategy of some sort. We were reminded that for those to whom much has been given, much is required. It also struck us that, in the past, we'd had a scattershot approach that wasn't very thoughtful, or efficient. We were giving money here and there and everywhere, and it was adding up quickly.

FOCUSED PHILANTHROPY

We had no overall plan. No real focus or strategy. And we weren't doing much research on the charities and organizations we were giving to. So, in 1994, Myrna and I established a family foundation with the more specific goals to promote the three pillars we decided were the most meaningful to our family: education and entrepreneurship, health care, and the arts.

In the following years, through the foundation, we financed construction of a Christian high school in Dallas, plus campaigns benefiting Southern Methodist University (SMU) and the Dallas Symphony Orchestra, as well as an entrepreneurial center at my alma mater, Wilfrid Laurier. Myrna also supported the Dallas Alzheimer's Association, and they recognized her efforts by establishing the Myrna D. Schlegel/AWARE scholarship for nursing students specializing in gerontology care.

Through our non-profit foundation we have supported the Students in Free Enterprise (SIFE), the Salvation Army, the Cox School of Business at SMU, and the Library of Congress's James Madison Council, which has programs that enhance the library's collection and enable greater access to it.

I've apparently become better at philanthropy than I ever expected to be because a few years ago I was inducted into the Texas Philanthropy Hall of Fame. I've also been honored to receive the Tom Landry Award for Excellence and Volunteerism and the Outstanding Philanthropist Award from the Association of Fundraising Professionals.

I've had a very fulfilling life thanks to my career as an entrepreneur, and as a result, a lot of my focus is on encouraging others to start their own businesses. In 2002, we joined with my alma mater Wilfried Laurier University in Waterloo, Ontario, to create the Schlegel Centre for Entrepreneurship and Social Innovation.

My wife and business partner has her own favorite charities and non-profits. Myrna's family is very musical, and she has always loved classical music. Her brother was a professional baritone, and her sister-in-law is director of musical studies at the University of Toronto, as well as the chorus master for the Canadian Opera Company.

Myrna also served on the Dallas Symphony board and very quickly became chairman of the board. This position gave her the ability to work on balancing a big non-profit's budget, a job with which she became very familiar.

One of the organizations closest to my heart is the Horatio Alger Association of Distinguished Americans, which inducted me into its membership in 2008. This great group honors those who have overcome adversity to achieve success and the American dream, and then are willing to reach back and help others. Receiving this award from the U.S. Supreme Court Justice Clarence Thomas was one of the highlights of my life.

The Horatio Alger Association is dedicated "to the simple but powerful belief that hard work, honesty, and determination can conquer all obstacles." There are currently more than 300 living members, including 10 from Canada.

I particularly enjoy the fact that Horatio Alger members support promising young people by providing more than $20 million in scholarships each year in North America, helping more than twenty-seven thousand students over the years.

Myrna and I have made many friends within this outstanding organization, and we've even invited a few existing friends to be inducted.

It has been humbling and also rewarding to be recognized by many different organizations for the charitable and philanthropic work Myrna and I have been fortunate enough to do. The greatest honor of my life was being named the Dallas Father of the Year in 2002!

We have supported a wide range of causes and organizations, but our overall approach is to look for those that follow the concept of the proverb that says, "Give a man a fish and he will eat for a day. Teach a man how to fish and you feed him for a lifetime."

In other words, we don't believe that simply giving money or objects to someone or some group is the best approach. We would rather support those who are striving to elevate their lives or the lives of others by being better and doing better.

That can mean offering financial support for scholarships and grants, but it can also mean offering guidance, teaching a skill, and helping individuals learn self-sufficiency so they can survive and thrive on their own.

This is a family foundation and our grown children also can make contributions from it. They all have different interests, and we encourage them to find causes and organizations they are passionate about. One of them may focus on supporting aspiring and working artists. Another may be especially passionate about helping the homeless and hungry find both temporary shelter and meals, as well as paths to self-sufficiency.

We are all trying to be more strategic in our giving to make sure our philanthropy has the positive impact that we want it to have. Our financial advisors say there are a few key steps in the process for strategic philanthropy.

ENTREPRENEURIAL APPROACHES TO PHILANTHROPY

Entrepreneurs give more to non-profits and volunteer more than their financial peers from other fields, according to a study done by Fidelity Investments. They found that on average, the median annual gift from entrepreneurs is 50 percent higher than that of non-entrepreneurs. They also reported that two-thirds of entrepreneurs volunteer two or more hours a month, compared with just more than half of non-entrepreneurs.

They also posited that entrepreneurs are much more likely than their financial peers to feel that philanthropy is an important part of their lives. The report noted that entrepreneurs are far more likely to make giving a family tradition and to see the connection between volunteering and professional success.

The other interesting aspect of this Fidelity study was the finding that most entrepreneurs apply their business skills to their philanthropic efforts, meaning they are very much hands-on, creative in their approaches, and keen on making sure that their money and their efforts result in the maximum results for their targeted charities.

Now, I read somewhere that the way to create a $1 billion company is to solve a huge societal problem. I like to think that my solar energy pavers and our Silverwood master-plan starter home project will take us in that direction. I've come to believe that the best philanthropy is driven by entrepreneurial approaches to problem-solving.

Business entrepreneurs have the skills, drive, and mindsets to take philanthropy to a higher level. We can help create sustainable and self-sufficient organizations that address society's greatest needs. The first step is to make them profitable. We can do this by investing in start-ups and supporting them as they grow into successful enterprises that can provide long-term solutions to issues like poverty, homelessness, disease, and lack of access to education, or other needs.

Imagine what entrepreneurs could do if we thought of the homeless or jobless as potential workers for an organization that trained them, paid them, and helped them find opportunities to rise out of poverty while finding meaningful work, maybe for non-profits around the world in need of workers?

Entrepreneurs are skilled at finding opportunities everywhere they look. I encourage you to practice philanthropy in the same way, by thinking about what the opportunities are for developing sustainable businesses that help alleviate poverty, hunger, disease, homelessness, and lack of access to education.

Successful entrepreneurs are also typically strong when it comes to recruiting people with a wide range of complementary talents, knowledge, and skills. This would prove useful in building a for-profit business that tackles a pressing social need.

I am biased, without a doubt, but I think entrepreneurs can bring transformational change to the world of philanthropy. We spend our careers serving customers and their needs. We only succeed if we are successful in doing that. I believe that we could be just as successful targeting societal needs and finding long-term solutions with sustainable business models.

PHILANTHROPY PREP 101

As I was writing this book, I lost a friend, and the world lost a wonderful entrepreneur and one of America's great philanthropists who serves as a role model for all of those who strive to make the world a better place. I met Walter Scott, Jr. through our membership in the Horatio Alger Association of Distinguished Americans. He was a legend in the construction, telecommunications, and energy industries, creating a $100 billion company that is now known as Berkshire Hathaway Energy.

Walter, who lived in Omaha, Nebraska, and maintained a low-profile throughout his life, believed in supporting worthwhile causes with a focused mission. In an interview for use in a Horatio Alger publication, he outlined three points that he wanted his children to always remember.

1. *Your greatest asset is your health. Don't do anything to jeopardize it.*

2. *The greatest thing you can acquire is an education. No one can take that away from you.*

3. *The greatest thing you can do is be a giver. The world already has enough takers.*

I think Walter's points are important for us all to keep in mind. My own guidance for entrepreneurs is to approach your philanthropic efforts with the same zeal, determination, and due diligence that you use when launching a start-up, so that you focus your efforts on causes and organizations you care about deeply. Here are a few bits of advice I have for entrepreneurs interested in giving back to their communities for the benefit of others.

1. Take time to think about what causes are important to you.

Once we decided to be more focused in our philanthropy, Myrna and I identified areas that we are most concerned and passionate about, while leaving room for others that might come to our attention, of course. We advised our children to do the same when getting involved, giving from the family foundation, or from their own funds.

We've always involved our children in our businesses, so it makes sense to get them involved in our philanthropy, too. They have their own fields of expertise and their own interests and concerns now, and we encourage them to practice thoughtful giving.

2. Check the credentials and the operating practices of any organization or individuals you target for your donations or your time.

It is sad to say, but not all non-profit charitable groups are well-run or ethical in their practices. There are some that spend most of the donated money for telemarketing, fundraisers, and mailers. A few nasty ones spend 90 percent on fundraising alone. I've seen media reports that say more than $1 billion of donated funds are misspent by non-profits.

We have learned to investigate any new recipient of our foundation's funds to make sure that the donation goes where it is meant to go, and not to high executive salaries or administrative costs that might include expensive meals, hotels, or travel.

Fortunately, there are several very good resources out there that monitor them on a regular basis and provide ratings and recommendations. I encourage you to use their services whenever you are looking at donating to a group, and to check at least once a year to make sure your money is being spent wisely.

Charity watchdog groups like the BBB Wise Giving Alliance caution donors that con artists sometimes create non-profit groups with names that sound like those of legitimate or highly ranked charities but are really scams or low-ranked.

One of the more egregious examples of this was a California charity for veterans that raised millions of dollars through a telemarketing service, but more than 90 percent of all donations were kept by the telemarketer—for more than three decades. In fact, the telemarketer continued soliciting funds even though the veteran's group was three year's delinquent on its state registration. An investigation found that the veteran's group never received more than ten cents for every dollar raised by the telemarketer.

Charity monitoring groups usually have a list of standards for those non-profits that they recommend. Their measures include strong conflict-of-interest policies, as well as a requirement that at least 65 percent of their total expenses be directed to charitable programs, and no more than 35 percent of total contributions spent on fundraising. But even 35 percent is still too much. The Salvation Army is one of the most efficient large charities in the world, with the lowest cost and highest flow-through (82 percent) to their programs. Many church fundraisers, including the Mennonite

Central Committee relief sale, are up to 100 percent more efficient because all their work is done by volunteers.

My advice is to check the recipients of your donations at least once a year with the BBB Wise Giving Alliance (www.give.org), Charity Navigator (www.charitynavigator.org), Charity Watch (www.charitywatch.org), and even *Consumer Reports* (www.consumerreports.org), which ranks charities.

For example, *Consumer Reports* recommends that you check out smaller, lower-profile non-profits with these ratings groups: GiveWell, (www.givewell.org), GlobalGiving, (www.globalgiving.org), and ImpactMatters (www.impactmatters.org).

3. Consider the impact of your giving on your taxes.

As much as I like helping out deserving individuals with direct donations, being able to save income tax dollars allows you to give even more to additional charities. When you give to most non-profits, you can claim the donations as a tax-deductible expense. Philanthropy watchdog groups advise you to make sure your donations are tax-deductible by checking with the targeted group or on the website of the Internal Revenue Service (IRS). Your accountant will certainly be appreciative!

4. Give from the heart.

One of our favorite charitable organizations is close to our hearts because of family ties that go back several generations to our family in Canada. We admire the Mennonite Economic Development Association (MEDA) because it invests in programs that enhance the lives of people in need by helping them become more self-sufficient. We've found that this group gives a great return on donated dollars.

MEDA is an international economic development organization whose mission is to create business solutions from poverty. I also like this group because it was founded by entrepreneurs, and it partners with people in need to help them start or grow businesses in developing regions of the world.

This organization seeks to alleviate poverty by teaching men and woman how to help themselves and giving them access to investments and environmentally friendly technologies and practices. They've done this by investing and advising entrepreneurs since 1953, working in 62 countries, and helping 103 million families.

We believe our thoughtful donations to organizations like this can have an impact that will outlive us all.

Another one of our favorite charities is one that packs a punch because it was founded by our longtime friend Chuck Norris. The martial arts world champion, actor, and philanthropist started KickStart Kids in 1990 to teach character to schoolchildren through karate, which he believes helps instill in them core values, including discipline and respect.

Chuck also strives to help children achieve their greatest potential by having black-belt martial arts instructors present daily classes and deliver daily in-school lessons that create a positive impact on students, their families, schools, and communities.

This year, more than ten thousand students are enrolled in sixty-two schools across the state of Texas. So far, more than 100,000 students have benefitted from this one-of-a-kind, life-changing program.

5. Look for need wherever you are working.

Most entrepreneurs have clients and projects in many locations, which means they also have the opportunity to not just make money, but to make a difference in many places. I mentioned the social impact entrepreneurism of Dallas-based decorator Trisha Wilson in an earlier chapter. This world-renowned interior designer did many high-profile landmark and luxury projects on the African continent over the years, including the Palace of the Lost City, the Zimbali Forest Lodge, and The Blue Train.

Trish also worked on the Oprah Winfrey Leadership Academy for Girls in South Africa. She grew so fond of the region, Trisha built a home there called Izingwe Lodge, in the middle of the Welgevonden Game Preserve, in the beautiful North Province of South Africa. Yet her most impactful project may well be the private school she built and the large clinic she renovated and continues to support in the impoverished Limpopo province north of Johannesburg.

Trisha, who supports many other local, national, and international organizations through her Wilson Foundation, advises other entrepreneurs interested in philanthropy to keep in mind that the operations side of non-profits often are often overlooked, but deserve their support, as well.

"Many big givers want to see their names on buildings, but there are other less sexy places where they can make a big difference," she said. "I'm not big on buying tables and big gala events for charities. I think my giving is better spent on the operations areas of a school or clinic because that will help keep them alive and serving their students and clients."

6. Give your time and talents, too.

As Trisha and Myrna and I have found, giving money may not be as important as contributing your time and expertise to non-profits and worthy organizations.

Follow-through is equally important. "When we give scholarships, we don't just hand it to an institution and walk away," Trisha says. "We follow the students, often for years and even into adulthood, mentoring them and giving additional help such as helping with housing and transportation costs, as well as other guidance when necessary."

She notes that while most recipients thrive, the donor has to face reality and know that some of the seeds they plant may not flourish, despite all of their good intentions and efforts.

"You have to be prepared for heartbreak, too," Trisha says. "We have one person in South Africa whom we've been helping since the age of three. We got him out of an abusive household, and helped him through grade school and high school, but at this point, he lacks initiative and hasn't found a direction for his life. I have not given up on him yet, but I am waiting for him to become more motivated and focused."

Philanthropy also includes stepping up and providing leadership when there is a need. Most charities need leaders willing to build the organization and expand fundraising efforts, as well as the philanthropic outreach.

Myrna will tell you also that leading a non-profit organization requires even more finesse and diplomacy than running a business.

"When leading an organization staffed mostly by volunteers, who are giving their time and sharing their talents, you can't issue orders and directives like you might in a business," she says. "You have to build consensus and be more cognizant of their feelings and their motivation for being involved."

Even men and women who have served as top executives at major businesses have to learn to adjust their management styles when leading a non-profit that relies mostly on a volunteer staff. I've seen reports that more than a third of those who volunteer at non-profits don't return to give more of their time after the first year. One study said that results in lost labor worth $38 billion to charitable organizations.

Myrna learned to use a different strategy with volunteers at the Dallas Symphony, compared to paid workers in our nursing and retirement centers. She also discovered that there can be a big difference between managing older volunteers and younger volunteers who haven't had as much real-world experience.

My wife found it helps to view the volunteer workers as valuable resources who often have skills and experience that would make them highly paid employees if they were on the payroll. Many have

IT skills, legal and accounting backgrounds, and fundraising and management expertise that allows them to make major contributions to any non-profit.

It is also true that many older volunteers, especially, often are also donors to those organizations where they give their time. Many non-profits view their volunteers as valuable additions who keep the paid staff from being overworked, serve as mentors to younger staff, and can fill in for those on vacation or leave.

Myrna also discovered that her volunteers were great assets because they knew the community well and were effective at recruiting donors and other volunteers while also promoting the organization on social media and in their social circles. Wise leadership of volunteers includes making sure their talents and experience are fully tapped so that they feel valued, fulfilled, and well-matched to their assignments.

Asking a retired lawyer or CPA to send out mailers or perform other office chores is not the best possible use of valuable talent and will likely result in their loss to the organization if continued for long periods. Volunteers, like paid employees, enjoy their work more if they are allowed to become fully engaged mentally and physically. I've heard stories of retired professionals serving as volunteers who have made suggestions that have saved organizations millions and helped make them better serve their clients.

Volunteers should be recognized on a regular basis for their contributions. Some organizations list the hours worked by each volunteer in their annual reports. A few non-profits even put a dollar value on their time and efforts to show appreciation.

Some non-profit leaders are reluctant to invest in training volunteers for fear that they won't work often enough or long enough to justify the investment. Many volunteers never receive any formal training, and all too often paid staff members aren't provided any kind of training in how to manage volunteers. Myrna and I have come to believe that if you provide adequate training to both, it will pay off in the long run because your volunteers will feel more appreciated and put in more hours.

SUPPORTING STRIVERS

Every now and then, we run across someone who simply deserves a break and we decide to step in with our support and encouragement. Recently, Myrna and I met a young lady who had risen above difficult circumstances. She comes from an impoverished family and faced adversities that we can't even imagine. Yet she stood out academically and won a scholarship to a good university.

When we learned that she was driving eighty miles every day because she couldn't afford to live on campus, we decided to help her with housing and education costs as a reward. We wanted to help her build a new life. In truth, she didn't need any motivation. She already had that. Now that she can live on campus, in a sorority house, she has become a leader active in several campus volunteer groups. We have enjoyed seeing her flourish and grow in that environment, as well as enhance her leadership skills.

We are grateful that we've been able to make a difference in this outstanding young lady's life and our support of her education is an example of my favorite type of philanthropy, which has an entrepreneurial aspect to it. Myrna and I encourage our children and other entrepreneurs and aspiring entrepreneurs to serve their community and deserving individuals by finding sustainable solutions that go beyond simply writing a check.

My friend Jim Keyes is another philanthropist who believes that those of us who have achieved success in life should accept responsibility for helping others do the same. Jim helped start a great charity called "Education is Freedom." In 2002, as CEO of 7-Eleven, Jim launched Education is Freedom (EIF) with a big splash at Radio

City Music Hall, and Myrna and I attended to help celebrate. The inspiration for EIF was an interesting story.

I will let Jim tell it:

"As a public company, 7-Eleven was always trying to improve shareholder return and profitability. The charitable budget was being challenged by the board. They wanted me to make cuts. At the time we were spending hundreds of thousands a year but spread across many well-deserving causes. We had no focus or no measurable benefit. I really attacked this challenge. I tried to think of ways to show a benefit or even a measurable return on our contribution dollar investment.

"Our corporate focus was on training, education, and minority programs (representing a big part of our customer base and workforce). I decided to test a program that focused on public schools to 'grow our own' future employees by providing mentorship and scholarships to underprivileged public-school kids. "After a small test with two schools in Dallas, we founded Education is Freedom. Our vision was to put a counselor in each public school to show students the pathway from high school to college and ultimately to a career, providing mentoring, advice, curriculum guidance, and help with scholarship applications.

"The test program started in Dallas ISD and is now in most of the Dallas public schools, and partially funded by the school district. We have successfully changed many lives with countless stories of students who would have never gone to college.

"One of my favorites, Adan Gonzales, was the first in his family to go to college. By his own admission he would have otherwise been a gang member. Instead, he went on to graduate from Georgetown, went to on to Harvard for a masters and now is back in Dallas teaching in Dallas ISD.

"In Dallas alone, we have had over 175,000 students go through the program since inception and we have raised or given over $465 million in scholarship assistance. This is just the beginning. We have the opportunity to do so much more and to continue changing lives."

Chapter Ten

PAVING THE WAY

In November of 2018, the stage was set for my angels to step in once again to save me from yet another near disaster.

I went in for my annual checkup, which is typically a quick and painless process. As usual, the doctor said everything looked good, and then he sent me on to my last stop on the checkup tour, for my five-year CT body scan.

It's a ten-minute scan in the can. No big deal!

Except this time.

The next day, my doctor called.

"We need to talk about a shadow on your lung that showed up in the CT," he said.

That didn't sound good.

"I want you to see our thoracic specialist tomorrow," he added.

That sounded even worse.

The thoracic surgeon said that there was a shadow that looked like a tumor on my upper right lobe.

"I'd say there is a 75 percent chance that it's cancer, but we need to do a biopsy," he said.

They did the biopsy, but they still were unable to be absolutely sure whether it was cancer or not because they had difficulty getting a good sample. I was hoping for proof one way or another. They didn't have it. Even so, the surgeon wanted to operate and remove the tumor, which is what surgeons do.

I decided to get a second opinion before going under the knife. This time, I went to a renowned head thoracic surgeon of a large, well-known hospital.

"Mr. Schlegel," he said, "I'm 90 percent sure this is a cancerous tumor. We need to take out that upper right lobe."

Both physicians asked me if I'd ever been a smoker, which was interesting. I have never been a smoker. In fact, I'm the guy who had a restriction against hiring smokers. So maybe this lump was the revenge of all the smokers I wouldn't hire?

I didn't really blame the doctors, but no one seemed to know the source of this lump. The doctors explained that there are many ways a non-smoker can get lung cancer. Radon gas is one of the other big causes. Frequent exposure to secondhand smoke, asbestos, arsenic, diesel fumes, and air pollution are others. Or it can be the result of a gene mutation. Apparently, 20 percent of lung cancers are found in people who have never smoked!

I guessed I found one of those triggers because I had something that looked like a tumor.

"The good news is that you're a healthy guy otherwise, so I don't think this will slow you down much," the surgeon said. "You may not ever be an Olympic swimmer or mountain climber after we remove that lobe, but you can still work out and be a good entrepreneur."

I was thinking I would have a couple of weeks to make up my mind when the surgeon said, "Let's take it out on Thursday," which was two days later. I underwent a five-hour surgery to remove that whole lobe. They told me everything went well, there was no cancer, and it would take a couple weeks to fully recuperate.

That didn't happen. My registered-nurse wife was watching over me in the intensive care recovery room that night when she noticed that my blood pressure kept dipping, and that set off alarms in her mind.

"I think he's bleeding internally," she said to the intensive care nurses. They called the surgeon in the middle of the night to come back in.

The doctor confirmed, "There is a problem. You *are* losing blood! My team is on the way and we are going back in!"

Easy for him to say. It was *my* body that he was going back into!

They dragged me onto a gurney and hauled me back in for another five hours of surgery to plug all the leaks. I will never forget that ride down to the operating room with my son by my side.

Eight hours after my initial surgery, I was back on the operating table. This surgery was much scarier than the first. I lost a lot of blood before and during the operation.

My angels were looking out for me this time, however, including my number one angel, Myrna. My family and friends unleashed a nonstop prayer bombardment, calling on all the active angels and maybe even some who came out of retirement. Their prayers definitely worked.

I was out of the hospital in ten days, and the doctors said I was cancer free. They did leave a few tubes in me, but two weeks later, I broke free and hit the road with my son-in-law to go to a business seminar in New Orleans, where we joined my son and other son-in-law and two of our business managers. We were back working as a team again!

The doctors wouldn't let me fly, so we drove eight hours there and eight hours back. Hey, it wasn't nearly as long as the drive back to Canada that we did every other week for six years with our children, the nanny, and Axle the dog.

Myrna and the kids were not at all happy with my refusal to stay home and go through a lengthy recuperation period, but I pointed out that the doctors decided the lump in my lung wasn't cancer.

Myrna countered that with, "They are still trying to figure out what it was."

"Well, in the meantime, I can't just sit around," I said.

That was the truth then, and now.

I'm not much for just sitting around. I'm an entrepreneur, after all, and I want to leave a legacy to inspire, motivate, and guide future generations of entrepreneurs. I'm hoping that more than a few of my children and grandchildren will be among them.

And maybe you, too!

As I was writing this final chapter, I celebrated my seventieth birthday. My father died at the age of sixty-nine, my brother at sixty-eight, so I figure I'm in unchartered territory. Every day is a blessing from here on out, and I intend to make the most of each one of them.

I intend to follow the guidance of Benjamin Franklin, who wrote: "If you would not be forgotten as soon as you are dead, either write something worth reading, or do something worth writing."

I want to keep creating and growing businesses that benefit my customers, our community, and the world. And I want to spend as much time as possible with my ever-growing family, loving them and being loved by them.

LIVING IT EVERY DAY

I began this chapter reflecting on a major health crisis that certainly made me look back on my life and my legacy at a later stage in my life. But our legacies are created across our lifetimes. It's never too late to be a better person, but we should live every day striving to create a legacy that inspires and enriches the lives of everyone we interact with.

If you keep your legacy in mind, you are bound to be better and do better. I have a few other suggestions for leaving a powerful and inspiring legacy.

1. *Help others find success and success will find you.*

2. *Treat every person you meet as a gift and a resource.*

3. *Be a source of support and encouragement, and you will never lack for either.*

4. *Do not take failures personally, because over the long term, they may prove to be blessings, or they may lead to blessings.*

5. *Wealth is not a burden, but it is a responsibility. To whom much is given, much is required.*

6. *Pursue your passions, but know there are many paths to fulfillment.*

7. *Be kind instinctively. Forgive instantly. Give thanks habitually.*

8. *Opportunity is the greatest gift. Do not waste any chance to either receive it or give it.*

9. *Know that there is a higher power, and He will provide angels in your life.*

Here are some of my favorite lessons to remember:

1. *PEP: Persistence, Entrepreneurship/Education, and Passion with a Purpose*

2. *Be good, work hard!*

3. *No matter how far you are down the wrong road, turn around!*

4. *Big Hairy Audacious Goals (Serve as targets, but your budget should be more practical. The BHAGs are part of a long-term vision).*

5. *You gotta be on the corner when the bus stops.*

6. *If you can't say anything nice about someone, don't say anything at all!*

7. *Safety first, then quality, and then quantity.*

MAKING A DIFFERENCE

Your legacy is what remains of you after you've departed from the physical world, or as Shakespeare put it with more eloquence, "When we have shuffled off this mortal coil."

Your legacy then, includes the stories that are told about you, the impression and influence you've had on the lives of others, the feelings experienced when your name is brought up, or the way your work is recognized. It is how you treated others, the values you lived by, and the businesses you built that outlived you, the books you wrote, and the art you created.

Most of all, it is the hearts you touched.

I have had my ups and downs as an entrepreneur. There have been some deep valleys and scary moments, but, thankfully, my heavenly and earthly angels have watched out for me, and I hope to leave behind a strong foundation for my descendants to build upon.

What they do with it, and the type of people they become, is dependent on the decisions they make based on the values they live by.

So, really, what is most important isn't the material wealth you accumulate over a lifetime so much as the quality of your character and the power of the values you pass on to the next generations.

I doubt that many entrepreneurs think much about their legacy when they are starting out. Maybe only a few more consider it as they grow their businesses and experience success. In truth, most don't give their legacies much thought until they are late into their careers and preparing to retire.

That is understandable, but my hope is that you will start thinking about the legacy you want to leave right now, if you haven't done so already. I say that because I believe knowing where you want to end up—and how you want to be remembered—will make you do better and be better as you pursue your career.

When Myrna and I started a family together, we had strong feelings about the values we wanted to instill in our children. We thought a lot about what kind of men and women we wanted them to grow up to be.

Our goal was to teach them values through our words, but mostly through our actions. In every way possible, we let them know they were loved and supported. Yet, we also taught them to find what they loved to do and then to work hard to build their own businesses and careers.

So, with our children, who are certainly part of our legacy as parents, we worked toward that long-term goal of encouraging them to be independent, focused on achievement, family-oriented, and caring human beings. And I think we've succeeded, at least from the evidence so far.

Our work on building a legacy is far from done, but the values that Myrna and I learned from our own parents—it has been said that our parents live inside of us—and our extended families still guide us. As long as we stick with their values, I think we will be on track.

When I think of the legacy left by my own father, this is one of the stories that comes to mind:

Dad had a friend who was also a farm equipment dealer. We traded for a new tractor with him, and it turned out to be a terrible deal. The tractor never worked properly. My father was typically very even-keeled and slow to anger, but I can remember him expressing considerable anger over this deal.

I felt his friend had taken advantage of him.

"Dad you've got to go over there and give him a piece of your mind," I said. "I want to go with you to see this," I continued. "I want to be there when you tell him off."

So we went to the friend's dealership, but their conversation was not what I had expected, at all. My dad could not have been nicer to the guy. And the owner was nice to my father, too.

My father never raised his voice. He said quietly and politely, "The new tractor isn't working."

He then calmly explained the problem. After hearing him out, the farm equipment dealer replaced the tractor without any argument. My dad solved the problem without any harsh words or hurt feelings.

That story and the values it portrays is a big part of my father's legacy to me. One of the truths about leaving a legacy is that values are caught rather than taught. My father never sat me down and talked through that story as a lesson in life. He didn't have to. I absorbed it by observing him and his actions.

The underlying message in this example is an important one, especially for entrepreneurs. Most business in a capitalistic society is done on a transactional basis. You sell. I buy. I sell. You buy. We both want to benefit and profit from the deal.

The entrepreneur survives through favorable transactions, making more than what is spent, hopefully! As a numbers guy, I can get swept up in the metrics of performance; key performance indicators like sales revenue cash flow net monthly recurring revenues, and similar measures found on spreadsheets.

I wrote about these measures earlier in the book. They are important for your business success, but not so much for your legacy. I certainly hope that when my friends and family gather for my wake, no one will stand up to talk about my skill with key performance indicators, or any material wealth I left behind.

Instead, we try to leave a legacy that is not so much about the quality of the transactions in our lives, but the quality of our relationships. How we lived each and every day, and the good values that we lived by. Did we look for the best in others rather than the worst? Did we treat every person as someone with inherent worth, talents, and knowledge to share?

Did we look to "win" every interaction because we had a scarcity mentality, or did we look to create a win-win because we had an abundance mentality and believed there is success enough for all of us in this world? And did we act upon negative emotions by turning them into a positive force?

This was the lesson my father taught me in his transaction with the tractor dealer, which he turned into a modestly transformative experience—and a legacy that will be passed on for generations.

ACKNOWLEDGMENTS

I would like to thank my literary agent and good friend Jan Miller Rich of Dupree Miller & Associates for making this dream of a book come true. Special thanks to wordsmith Wes Smith who miraculously captured my rapid-fire words and guided them to these pages. Thanks also to the team at Post Hill Press.

All author proceeds from the sale of this book will go to philanthropic causes.